A Prolog Primer

Jean B. Rogers

University of Texas at Austin

ADDISON-WESLEY PUBLISHING COMPANY
Reading, Massachusetts • Menlo Park, California
Don Mills, Ontario • Wokingham, England • Amsterdam
Sydney • Singapore • Tokyo • Madrid • Bogota
Santiago • San Juan

Library of Congress Cataloging-in-Publication Data
Rogers, Jean B.
    A Prolog primer.

    Includes index
    1. Prolog (Computer program language)   I. Title.
QA76.73.P76R64   1986   005.13'3   85-22846
ISBN 0-201-06467-7

Reprinted with corrections October, 1986

Dedicated to my children,
Dennis and Diane

PURPOSE

The purpose of *A Prolog Primer* is to teach the fundamental skills and concepts needed for Prolog programming. Prolog is a computer programming language that has recently come to the forefront in computer science because of its potential for use in artificial intelligence programming, in information management systems, and in education. Prolog was created in 1972 by the Groupe d'Intelligence Artificielle at the Universite d'Aix Marseilles. The name, Prolog, is derived from "programming in logic"; the model upon which Prolog is built is that of formal logic. In the years since its development, the Prolog language has been expanded and improved and has gained favor for a number of computer applications.

A Prolog program is a way of representing knowledge. By using Prolog, not only can we represent facts, but we can also represent implications of fact, conclusions based on the facts and implications, and strategies for discovering conclusions. Prolog can be used for creating knowledge-based systems known as expert systems, in which a computer emulates the expertise of a human. Expert systems not only report conclusions but may also hold a dialog with the person who is using the system, asking questions and explaining how it reached its conclusions. Prolog can also be used in natural language processing. Natural language processing involves taking human communication and analyzing it to deduce the knowledge it represents.

Prolog is also gaining popularity for use in education. Some schools use Prolog as an instructional tool and others teach Prolog programming. Since Prolog is easy to learn, even students in elementary school can enjoy using it. Learning Prolog provides experience using a computer as well as experience looking carefully at knowledge about a subject and learning to express it in a formal system.

One characteristic of Prolog makes it appropriate for education as well as for artificial intelligence programming. Prolog is good for dynamic, free exploration. The interactive, responsive nature of the Prolog system encourages experimentation and discovery. This flexibility allows the programmer to develop the problem analysis while the program evolves.

APPROACH

The instruction in *A Prolog Primer* is oriented not only toward teaching the Prolog language but more importantly toward helping the reader understand how to think about the programming process for Prolog. Prolog is a declarative language, quite different from most of the currently popular languages. A Prolog program is a set of statements, declaring what is known to be true about the problem to be solved. The programming activity requires writing those statements in a form Prolog can use.

This book has a practical rather than a theoretical orientation. Prolog has a theoretical basis in logic but the language can be learned and used as a pragmatic tool. Whenever possible, the examples in the book have been chosen to represent effective solutions to typical problems. Appendix B lists references for further reading, many of which provide a more formal, theoretical discussion of Prolog.

Currently, there are a number of versions of Prolog available. They differ not in terms of the concepts they use but only in the way the programs are written down. Throughout the main part of this book, one version of Prolog is used consistently in the examples and the explanations. That version is Standard DECsystem-10/20 Prolog. Appendix C contains the form for three other common versions, C-Prolog, micro-PROLOG and SIMPLE. In the appendix, the parallel forms are given on a chapter by chapter basis, matching the examples in the book. Thus, a person who has available a different version of Prolog can use the information in Appendix C to modify examples from the book to run on the available system.

AUDIENCE

The audience for whom this book was written includes mature learners who are neither experienced in computer programming nor particularly sophisticated in mathematics. The examples throughout the first eight chapters are non-mathematical and generally related to "real world" rather than computer science problems. No computing background is assumed for this audience, so the book attempts to provide the computer system context needed. For specific details of specific systems, however, readers are pointed at other sources of information (such as system manuals) at the appropriate time.

This book is also an effective introduction to Prolog for people already quite familiar with computer programming. The appendixes, indexes and examples will facilitate the transfer of knowledge from earlier programming experience to Prolog. The experienced programmer is warned, however, that some new thinking is required for Prolog. The introduction to Part II has been specifically provided to help people adapt their experience in programming procedural languages like Pascal and BASIC to programming in Prolog.

There are several instructional environments where *A Prolog Primer* would be appropriate as a textbook. Primary among them are courses in computing for students who are not computer science majors. For example, library science, mathematics, business and science courses that teach programming would be well served to teach Prolog.

Another instructional environment where this book could serve as a text is computer science classes where students have experience in procedural programming but need to be introduced to other programming models. For example, many current Survey of Programming Languages courses include Prolog.

A third learning environment is less formal: individuals who want an introduction to Prolog for their personal interest can use this book. Because answers to the exercises at the end of each section are included in the book, the independent learner has feedback available.

ORGANIZATION
A Prolog Primer is divided into two parts. The first, Tutorial, introduces all the ideas and notation for the core of Prolog. The second part, Advanced Topics, includes chapters about specific topics and discusses development of larger programs. Part I has extensive narrative explanation of fundamental Prolog concepts. It includes a chapter on making the transition from natural language to programming languages, three chapters on the components from which a Prolog program is written, and one chapter discussing the processing mechanism that underlies the use of a Prolog program.

Part II begins with an introduction that compares Prolog with other programming languages and points out the differences for the programmer who is moving from more common languages to Prolog. The next five chapters, the remainder of Part II, address specific topics: process control, input and output, built-in predicates, arithmetic and program development. The discussions in these chapters are concise and concentrate on specific detail.

PEDAGOGY
The pedagogic technique used is a spiral approach. Concepts are introduced and discussed briefly, then later discussed in greater depth. A number of analogies have been used to facilitate an intuitive understanding of the ideas that underlie the Prolog language.

This book is different from other programming texts, even in Prolog, in that number manipulation is left until late in the presentation. As a result, examples throughout the book are word-oriented rather than mathematical.

At the ends of Chapters 2-5 there are special sections called "Experimenting". In each of these, examples of computer interaction are shown. Readers are urged to use these examples as a basis for exploring the Prolog environment on their own.

At the ends of sections in all ten chapters, exercises are provided. Answers to these exercises are given in Appendix F. In some cases, alternate answers are given, but in all cases readers should bear in mind that there is almost always more than one way to write a computer program for a task and rarely a single way that can be declared "the best program". Each chapter also has review exercises, some of which are suggestions for programs.

The manuscript of *A Prolog Primer* has been used for instruction in courses with computer science and other graduate students, computer science undergraduates and undergraduates from non-computer science majors. Their feedback was a guiding factor in revisions for the book.

ACKNOWLEDGMENTS
My deepest gratitude goes to those students who gave me careful and thoughtful comments on the manuscript, to Jim Greer, Scott Roberts and John Conery, whose helpful suggestions did much to improve the book, and to my children and my friends who inspire and encourage me.

CONTENTS

PART

Tutorial

I

INTRODUCTION
How to Use This Book

A Prolog Primer can help you learn to program in Prolog whether or not you already know how to program in any computer language.

If you do not already know how to program, you will want to start your reading with Chapter 1 and follow through the whole first part, the Tutorial. When you get to the second part, the Advanced Topics, you may or may not want to read the introduction to that part. The introduction compares Prolog with other programming languages; the discussion of Prolog itself begins again in Chapter 6. Understanding the material in Part II does not depend on your learning the content of the introduction, but you may find it interesting.

If you already know how to program in some language other than Prolog, you may want to start your reading in this book with the introduction to Part II. Along with comparing the languages, the introduction points out several specifics where Prolog programming is different. After you have read the introduction to Part II, you may want to go directly on to the Advanced Topics there, or you may want to read parts of the Tutorial to learn more about particular facets of Prolog.

Whether you are new to programming or only new to Prolog, the listing of examples in the book should provide help in writing your own programs

Looking at Language

1

The purpose of this chapter is to help the learner:
- become aware of patterns in natural language.
- recognize the same semantic content in different syntactic form.
- realize that a specified form of expression can be used to generalize over a number of instances.
- specify which elements will be included in a set
  - by one definition.
  - by one definition and another.
  - by one definition or another.

1.1 NATURAL LANGUAGE AND STRUCTURED FORMS

Language is a way for human beings to communicate ideas. Computer programming languages provide communication between people and computers; natural languages, like English and Chinese, allow people to communicate with other people. Prolog is a programming language. The purpose of this book is to help the reader learn to be a programmer and be able to write Prolog programs. Our discussion of the specifics of Prolog, however, does not start until the second chapter of the book. In this first chapter, we will consider typical expressions we use in natural language and look at some ways to simplify those expressions.

We may look forward to the time when we can communicate with computers just as we do with another human, but right now, we are obliged to make some concessions. While Prolog is much more like natural language than are most other programming languages, we still must know how to provide information to Prolog in a regularized, simplified form. To develop that ability, we will look at some less formal forms and consider how they allow us to organize and generalize the communication we use in natural language.

Natural language is a rich, complex collection of vocabulary, sentence structure and interrelations between sentences. One example of the richness of natural language is that we have many ways of expressing the same idea:

He smashed his toe with the chair.
His injury resulted from dropping a chair on his toe.
His toe was injured by being smashed by a chair.
The chair smashed his toe.

These four sentences all tell of the same event, communicating approximately the same idea. Several key words are the same in each sentence, but their position and focus is different. The meaning of a sentence is called its *semantics*. The physical structure of the sentence is called its *syntax*. In natural language we use many different syntactic forms to communicate the same or only subtly distinct semantics. Using variety in language makes communication more interesting and more precise. In contrast, choosing one pattern and using it repeatedly makes communication simpler and more easily analyzed. In programming, and particularly in Prolog, only a few patterns are used.

General Forms

In the computer programming environment we choose patterns of expression that are simple and then use them repeatedly. Using patterns allows us to skip over some detail and still communicate the idea. We always try to select a form that not only provides a simplified pattern but also allows pieces of information to be grouped together. We can call a form that applies to a number of specific instances a generic form. For example, the smashed toe might be part of a list of injuries being reported.

reported	toe	smashed	chair
reported	finger	cut	glass
reported	knee	skinned	pavement

We can see a general pattern in this list and can use special notation to specify it.

reported < body part > < injury > < instrument >

The angle brackets < > simply indicate the general category rather than the specific items in each specific instance. Specifying this generic form helps organize several events into a group where all share some element of meaning.

When we simplify natural language expressions into these general forms, we lose much of its richness. It is often difficult to draw the fine line between acceptable simplifications and ones that destroy the validity of the statement. For example, we may make reference to something "people do" as a general rule or we may need to know the specific individuals who did a thing. To maintain validity of the information, we must give careful thought and attention to the context and purpose of the grouping.

Alternative Forms

The generic form above might be appropriate for reporting injuries but the smashed toe could well fit into a different pattern. In this case the generic form might be different.

smashed	toe	chair
smashed	crime	FBI
smashed	world-record	runner
smashed	< object >	< instrument >

Choosing the appropriate pattern to group a set of events or facts that belong in a set will depend on the larger context of the elements. By the same token, each individual person will have his or her own view of the larger context. While one person might prefer

smashed <object> <instrument>

another might prefer

smashed <instrument> <object>

or perhaps

<instrument> smashed <object>

None of these choices is inherently better than the others; individual people will have their own favorites. The important point to remember is that it is simplicity and consistency that facilitate communication. This is especially significant in the distilled natural language that is the basis for programming language.

EXERCISES 1.1

1. Write a general form for
   ate   soup   lunch
   ate   eggs   breakfast
   ate   beef   dinner
   ate   pie   dinner
2. Write a general form that adds which day's meal it was to the items above.
3. Specify three alternative general forms for the items in Exercise 2.
4. Organize the data from this paragraph into simplified items and then specify a generic form.

   This July I have to attend summer school for the first two weeks but the third week I can laze around. The last week in July I have to go to a meeting in New York.

1.2 SEMANTIC NETWORKS

A second way of looking at sentence structure is to use a diagram to represent the activity or relationship in the sentence. There are many kinds of diagrams that are used for this. One way of diagramming sentence information is called a semantic network.

A semantic network consists of words that are objects connected by arrows. Along each arrow a word or phrase is written that indicates the activity or relationship between the objects. For example,

Figure 1.1

Simple Semantic Networks

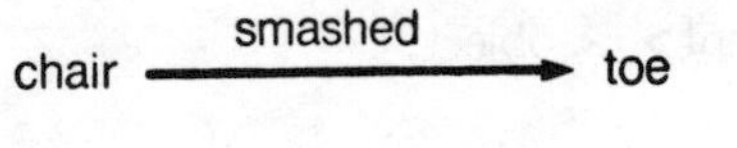

chair —— smashed ——▶ toe

glass —— cut ——▶ finger

Semantic networks are particularly useful when a single object appears in more than one sentence. A semantic network can show, for example, that a tornado smashed several buildings, as in Figure 1.2, or that several people eat pizza, as in Figure 1.3.

Figure 1.2

Network Centering on One Object

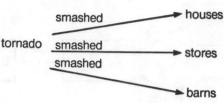

Figure 1.3

Alternative Network Centering on One Object

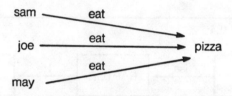

Certain types of relationships carry from one object to another. These relationships are called transitive because the relationship goes across intermediate objects. These, too, are shown well by semantic networks. For example,

Figure 1.4

Semantic Network of Transitive Relationship

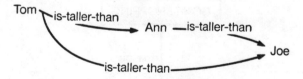

Semantic networks are particularly useful when we want to express a hierarchy of relationships. For example, objects are made up of other objects and are themselves components of other objects. This relationship can be denoted by ISPART, as in Figure 1.5.

Figure 1.5

Semantic Network of ISPART

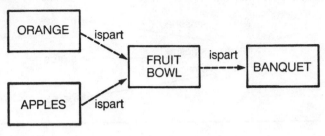

Another hierarchical relationship derives from the classification of objects. A relationship that shows classification can be written as ISA, like Figure 1.6.

Figure 1.6

Semantic Network of ISA

Sometimes it is clearer to have an event be the central object in a semantic network. An event is an abstract object that acts as the focus of some description. Figure 1.7 shows a semantic network based on a shopping trip.

Figure 1.7

Semantic Network Centered on an Event

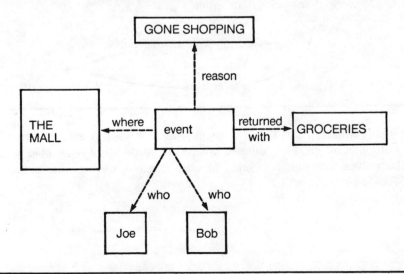

In every case in a semantic network, the arrow and the objects on each end of it express a relationship between the objects. The relationship is directed from one object to the other. We can consider the relationship and the object at the front of the arrow as an attribute and value of the attribute for the object at the base of the arrow. These attribute/value pairs give us a standardized form for representing knowledge about the object and provide a structure for gleaning information from the simplified representation of the knowledge.

EXERCISES 1.2

1. Draw a semantic network for the following examples.
   Joe, Jane and I went to the market.
   I talked Joe into getting watermelon and he talked Jane into it.
   I gave Jane some money so she could pay the bill.
   Joe gave me the car keys but I gave them back to him.
2. Write a natural language interpretation for these three semantic networks.

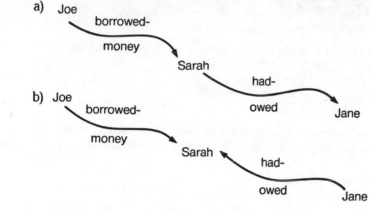

a) Joe
   borrowed-
   money
   Sarah
   had-
   owed
   Jane

b) Joe
   borrowed-
   money
   Sarah
   had-
   owed
   Jane

c)

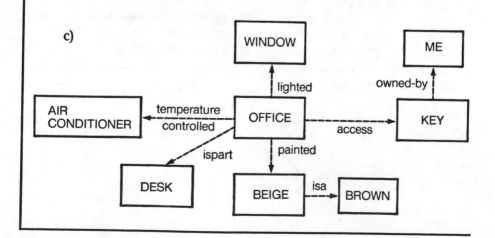

1.3 RECOGNIZING INSTANCES IN SETS

When one has various items, they can be grouped into sets of items. Often the grouping is done according to some general specification. The specification defines which items belong in the grouping and which ones do not. A generic form like those in Section 1.1 is one way of writing the definition for inclusion in the group. For example, assume we have a number of sentences such as the items:

1. Joe owns a bike.
2. Joe enjoys movies.
3. Jill owns three books.
4. Jill carpools with Sam.
5. Sam lives near Jill.
6. Sally owns a trumpet.
7. Jane lives near Jill.
8. Jane enjoys movies.
9. Sam enjoys movies.

Say we specified that sentences belong in a set if they contain similar information.

<who> owns <what>

Some of these sentences belong in the set and some do not. Sentences 1, 3, and 6 above make up the set for ownership. Another definition of a set could be

<who> enjoys movies

In this case only 2, 8 and 9 meet this requirement. We can say that the sentences that meet the requirement are *true* instances of the specifications.

Individuals in Sets

Another way of grouping the information in the nine sentences above is to look at the individual people identified in the sentences and group them according to what we know about them. We can call each group a set. In each of these cases, we can also specify which people do not belong in each set, based on the definition given.

Set	in	not-in
A People who own something	Joe Jill Sally	Jane Sam
B People who enjoy movies	Joe Jane Sam	Jill Sally
C People who carpool with Sam	Jill	Jane Joe Sam Sally
D People who live near Jill	Sam Jane	Joe Sally Jill

To specify who is *not* in one of these sets requires an important assumption: that these nine sentences about five people tell us all there is to know about everybody. Assuming that there is no further information about these people allows us to assume that if we do not know a fact, the fact is not true. This is called the closed world assumption. In this example, we also are avoiding self-references in facts. Thus we are concluding that Sam does not carpool with himself nor does Jill live near herself.

EXERCISES 1.3

1. Using the following sentences, write a generic form that divides the sentences into two groups.
   Sweaters keep you warm.
   Sweaters are good gifts.
   Long sox keep your feet warm.
   Sandals keep you cool.
   Shorts keep you cool, too.
   Flowers make a good gift.
2. Each sentence gives you information about an object. Pick those individual objects out of the sentences above and group them into three groups according to some characteristic stated in the sentences.
3. For each of your three groups above, list all the objects not in each group according to the sentences.

1.4 ONE DEFINITION AND ANOTHER

When we have individuals grouped into sets according to definitions, we can refine that grouping by finding items that meet two specifications. The group consists of items that meet one specification *AND* another specification. For example, in the sentences in Section 1.3, what people own something and enjoy movies? Only Joe meets both of these requirements.

In analyzing the grouping by definition or definitions, a useful tool is a graphic called a Venn diagram. Say we have the following three sets of people and their favorite leisure time activities.

A. Al, Bet, Cat, Den and Ed like reading.

B. Al, Bet, Fred and Gar like movies.

C. Bet, Den, Fred and Hal like plays.

In the Venn diagram in Figure 1.8, each circle encloses the names of people who belong in the specified set. The circles are drawn so that individuals appear in the circle for each grouping they belong to. Each person only appears once, however, so if that person is in two circles, the circles must overlap.

Figure 1.8

Venn Diagram of Three Sets

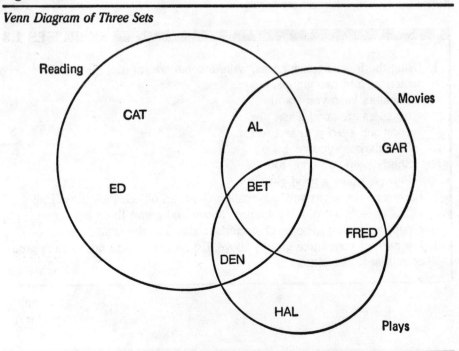

As a result, individuals who meet the specification of liking reading and of liking movies are shown in the overlap of those two circles. People who like all three (movies, reading, and plays) are in the overlap of all three circles. In this example only Bet meets this description. When we specify that each person must meet more than one requirement: that either maintains the grouping size or narrows down the number of people that are part of the grouping. In general, "and" adds restrictions for inclusion in a group, making the group more specific and often smaller.

1.5 ONE DEFINITION OR ANOTHER

In contrast to "and" which narrows down a grouping, "or" expands it. For an item to be part of a group defined by one requirement OR another, it only has to meet at least one, instead of both of the specifications. From the original Venn diagram, we can see "reading or movies" contains seven people, the grouping described by "reading or plays" contains everyone but Gar, and "movies or plays" includes everyone but Cat and Ed. Using "or" allows inclusion of items in a set on a more general but still defined basis. In general, "or" removes restrictions for inclusion in a group, making the group less specific and often bigger.

EXERCISES 1.4, 1.5

1. Draw a Venn diagram for these three sets.
    A. People who wear boots: Mike, Sam, Jo and Lou.
    B. People who ride bikes: Jo, Glen and Lou.
    C. People who jog: Ann, Char, Jo and Sam.
2. Identify the set A AND B. Who is in it?
3. Identity the set A AND B AND C. Who is in it?
4. Identify the set A OR B. Who is in it?
5. Who is in the set A OR B OR C?

SUMMARY

Any language has semantics, which is the meaning or the ideas being expressed, and syntax, which is the organizational structure of the language. Natural language is rich and complex, both in its semantics and its syntax. For computer programming, we want to simplify and regularize the syntax without losing too much of the semantics. To adapt natural language to programming, we use generalizations and patterns that simplify our expression of knowledge.

In this chapter we have seen several ways of representing knowledge in an organized and structured manner. Each of the ways makes use of some form or structure to carry information about the knowledge:
  • generic forms show patterns
  • semantic networks show relationships
  • sets and Venn diagrams show groupings.

Items of various kinds can be grouped according to specifications that define which instances are true and which are not true for the specification. The specifications can be joined by "and" which further narrows the grouping, or by "or" which broadens the grouping.

To program in Prolog, we will use precise forms of expression to convey information to the computer. The purpose of a program is to provide specifications that represent the knowledge we want to use. The precise forms, Prolog syntax, will be the communication medium.

EXERCISES CHAPTER 1

1. Identify the concept or concepts described by each phrase below.
    a) The part of a language that conveys meaning and ideas.
    b) The manner by which parts of a language are put together.
    c) The kind of language that (1) Prolog is; (2) English is.
    d) In sets, that which Venn diagrams represent graphically.
    e) A graphic method in which arrows and objects show attribute/value pairs.
    f) Assuming that a set of sentences includes all there is to know about some objects.
    g) A method to help us see patterns and groupings.
    h) In set specification, connectors that widen and narrow the specifications.
2. Draw a semantic network, a Venn diagram, and some generic forms based on this paragraph.
    Pavan had a party. John brought limeade and ice. Sally brought cheese and crackers, but Joe brought cheese too. Jan brought the same kind of cookies that she took to Mike's party last week.
3. Choose an event and describe it in several ways including some of the forms we discussed in this chapter. Compare the descriptions and choose the one you feel best communicates the information.

Prolog: To Define a World

The purpose of this chapter is to help the learner
- perceive a Prolog program as a self-contained world description.
- state Prolog facts.
- recognize the roles of constants and variables.
- ask Prolog questions for
    confirmation of facts.
    reporting of variable values.

2.1 PROGRAMMING LANGUAGES

A computer is a tool that can solve many different kinds of problems. For a computer to solve a particular problem, it must be given information about that problem. Programming languages are a way for people to communicate with a computer about the particular problem that is to be solved. The programming language is used to provide information about the problem and about the requirements for finding the solution to the problem. There are many different programming languages, but their role is always to communicate specifics of a problem to a computer.

Problems generally fall into one of a number of categories. For example, a problem like space navigation involves a lot of numeric calculations. Other problems, like printing transcripts for students, require taking a quantity of known information and arranging it in a form that people can easily understand. Because of the way programming languages have been designed, different ones match with certain types of problems. That is, the languages have the vocabulary and means of expression to communicate requirements that are typical of certain kinds of problems.

Prolog

Prolog is a programming language designed for a particular kind of problem. It is a convenient way to describe a self-contained world of knowledge. Tasks that can be carried out by following precise specifications can be done in a Prolog world that knows those specifications. For example, translation from one computer language to another can be done by a Prolog world that knows the translation rules. Another role for Prolog worlds is as an information resource. The world will provide selected information at the request of a person. This is the Prolog role we will focus on during the first part of this book.

The Prolog description of the world will consist of facts and rules. Once we have the world description, we can ask questions about that world. The questions we ask and the answers Prolog provides make using Prolog like holding a conversation with the computer, a conversation about the world described in the program.

The questions we ask will not be limited to requests for simple facts; Prolog will use the rules to combine facts about the world to find answers to complex questions. The questions themselves are descriptive. They describe requirements of the desired answer rather than specifying how to find out the answer. The facts and rules describe the world in the Prolog program; the questions describe the kinds of answers Prolog should provide from the world. Because of its character, Prolog is called a descriptive language. Neither the world nor the questions will give Prolog instructions about what actions should be carried out find the answer. That process is embedded in the Prolog system.

Of course, Prolog's answers will be constrained by the limits of the data it has been given in the description of the world. A Prolog program knows only about the world of knowledge that has been specified. Similarly, the description of the Prolog world need not match the world of our normal experience. If we choose to define a world in which "up" is the same as "down", Prolog will not object. Prolog allows a programmer to define a knowledge base and then explore that knowledge with questions.

A Base of Facts

A fundamental part of a Prolog description of a world is the facts it contains. Each fact is like a sentence, declaring a piece of information about one or more objects in the world. A collection of facts for Prolog is called a *base* or *database*. For example,

```
capital(texas,austin).
```

This Prolog fact shows that there is a relation between two objects, texas and austin.

In providing Prolog with a set of facts, we will follow rules as to how we write them. These rules, which are called *syntax* rules, are quite simple but very important. The name that defines the relationship appears first, then the names of the objects appear within parentheses, separated by a comma. Like a sentence, the fact ends with a period (.).

Syntax rules: facts

- relationship name first
- objects in parentheses, comma between
- period (full stop) at end

Example: `feeds(charlie,dog).`

The relationship name and the object names start with lower-case letters. This is to indicate to Prolog that these are names of specific objects and that the names will not change; they are called constants. Notice that there are no spaces within the fact. If we want to use a name that includes a space, we use an underscore in the space,

```
capital(new_york,albany).
```

These two examples use the same relationship name, capital. We can interpret these facts as meaning "The capital of Texas is Austin" and "The capital of New York is Albany". The order of the object names and the interpretation of the facts are freely chosen by the programmer who designs the facts. It is necessary, however, that the programmer, having made the choices, be consistent when using them within a program.

We could imagine, then, a set of 50 facts like these examples that specifies the capitals of all 50 states in the United States. In each case, the state name would come first and the capital-city name second. In the same base of facts, we can include other facts about the same objects

```
weather(texas,summer,hot).
```

or other completely independent objects

```
color(sox,green).
```

Sometimes only one object name appears within the parentheses of the fact. Then the name in front of the parentheses usually represents an attribute or characteristic of the object. For example

```
female(mary).
```

Prolog requires that an attribute or relationship and its objects, known also as the *predicate* and its *arguments*, maintain the same pattern throughout a program. Most commonly, predicates we use will have two or three arguments, but occasionally we will need more. The number of arguments for a predicate is known as its *arity*. For example, the capital predicate we have been using has an arity of two. In creating a base of facts, the programmer has responsibility for choosing the pattern and putting the names of objects in the appropriate position in a predicate. The pattern will be based on the meaning of the facts to the programmer. The meaning of the program is called the *semantics* of the program. Semantics stands in contrast to syntax, which as we said earlier, is the way the program is written down. The computer's processing is based on syntax, not semantics.

EXERCISES 2.1

1. Write Prolog facts based on these sentences.
   The book is on the table.
   The book is on the third shelf.
   John owns a dog.
   Jim owns a black dog.
2. What might these facts mean? Give at least two interpretations.
   ```
   mother(sarah,jane).
   father(joe,sam).
   ```
3. An old joke: Which is better, a ham sandwich or eternal happiness? Well, nothing is better than eternal happiness, and a ham sandwich is better than nothing. Therefore, a ham sandwich is better than eternal happiness. What does this have to do with Prolog facts?

2.2 QUERIES

When we have a base of facts, we can use Prolog to ask questions about the
world we have described in the database. A query follows the same syntax
rules that facts follow, but has a **?-** first. For example,

```
?- capital(oregon,salem).
```

This kind of question is a direct request for confirmation that a fact is in the
base that has been given. If we have a base that consists of a set of facts, one
giving the capital city for each of the 50 states in the United States, (see Figure
2.1) we could ask our question

```
?- capital(oregon,salem).
```

and Prolog would respond

```
yes
```

Figure 2.1

Facts — States and Capitals

```
capital(alabama,montgomery).          capital(montana,helena).
capital(alaska,juneau).               capital(nebraska,lincoln).
capital(arkansas,little_rock).        capital(nevada,carson_city).
capital(arizona,phoenix).             capital(new_hampshire,concord).
capital(california,sacramento).       capital(new_jersey,trenton).
capital(colorado,denver).             capital(new_mexico,santa_fe).
capital(connecticut,hartford).        capital(new_york,albany).
capital(delaware,dover).              capital(north_carolina,raleigh).
capital(florida,tallahassee).         capital(north_dakota,bismark).
capital(georgia,atlanta).             capital(ohio,columbus).
capital(hawaii,honolulu).             capital(oklahoma,oklahoma_city).
capital(idaho,boise).                 capital(oregon,salem).
capital(illinois,springfield).        capital(pennsylvania,harrisburg).
capital(indiana,indianapolis).        capital(rhode_island,providence).
capital(iowa,des_moines).             capital(south_carolina,columbia).
capital(kansas,topeka).               capital(south_dakota,pierre).
capital(kentucky,frankfort).          capital(tennessee,nashville).
capital(louisiana,baton_rouge).       capital(texas,austin).
capital(maine,augusta).               capital(utah,salt_lake_city).
capital(maryland,annapolis).          capital(vermont,montpelier).
capital(massachusetts,boston).        capital(virginia,richmond).
capital(michigan,lansing).            capital(washington,olympia).
capital(minnesota,st_paul).           capital(west_virginia,charleston).
capital(mississippi,jackson).         capital(wisconsin,madison).
capital(missouri,jefferson_city).     capital(wyoming,cheyenne).
```

If we asked

    `?- capital(oregon,portland).`

Prolog would respond

    no

If we asked

    `?- capital(ontario,toronto).`

Prolog would answer

    no

not because Toronto is not the capital of Ontario, but because that fact is not in the information we provided in our description to Prolog. We describe a world in our Prolog base. Prolog can only respond from the data in the base, answering "no" if a fact is not in that world.

Prolog checks to see if a fact exists in a database by using pattern matching. When asked a question, Prolog compares the first fact in the database with the expression given in the question. If it does not match, Prolog moves on to the next fact to try the match, and continues the process until one of two things happens. Either it succeeds in making the match, whereupon it reports "yes" or it checks the base clear through to the end and fails to find the match, so it reports "no". Prolog responds "no" to both the questions

    `?- capital(oregon,portland).`
    `?- capital(ontario,toronto).`

because it does not find matching facts in the base. Similarly, small typographic errors create completely different words. Thus,

    `?- capital(texas,asutin).`

would be answered

    no

Because Prolog is matching the pattern of the fact with the pattern in the question, details such as the spelling and the order of the object names must be attended to carefully.

Variables

We will sometimes want Prolog to check a piece of information against a data-base and report a "yes" or "no" to us. More frequently, however, we will want Prolog to fill in the name of an object that belongs in a relationship. To do this, we will again ask a question that contains the pattern we are looking for, but in the place of the name we want, we put a variable name. It is called a *variable* because it can stand in place of various objects. This variability is in contrast to the names which always refer to the same objects, *constant* names. In Prolog, we specify that a name is a variable by beginning the name with an upper-case letter. For example, in

```
?- capital(nevada,City).
```

City is a variable because it starts with an upper-case letter, C. If we asked this question of our base in Figure 2.1, Prolog would respond with

```
City = carson_city
```

We could as well have used any set of letters to represent the variable as long as the first is upper-case. Thus the question

```
?- capital(washington,XYZ).
```

will get the response

```
XYZ = olympia
```

Since XYZ is a variable, we can use it again

```
?- capital(california,XYZ).
```

to be told

```
XYZ = sacramento
```

Different people choose different kinds of words for variable names. Some people prefer a letter like X which is short and fast to use. Others prefer words like City, which may convey more meaning. Meaningful names help programmers make fewer mistakes.

We can use variables for any of the objects within the parentheses.

```
?- capital(State,pierre).
```

will get the response

```
State = south_dakota
```

and for

```
?- capital(State,charleston).
State = south_carolina
```

but for

```
?- capital(ontario,City).
```

we will be told "no" since the expression in the question has no match in our database, no matter what object the variable stands for. We are not limited to one variable in each question.

```
?- capital(State,City).
State = alabama   City = montgomery
```

In this case, any one of the facts in the database would match. Prolog responded with the first pair of objects it found, those in the fact at the beginning of the database.

While variables can stand in place of any of the object names in a fact, they cannot be used in place of the relationship name. Arguments may be variables, but predicates may not.

```
?- Connection(oregon,salem).
**^syntax error **
```

EXERCISES 2.2

1. Write Prolog facts to match these statements, then give examples of queries with variables that could be used with the facts.
   The book is on the table.
   The book is on the third shelf.
   John owns a dog.
   Jim owns a black dog.

2. Given these facts

```
owns(john,dog,midget).
owns(john,cow,jersey).
```

what will be the response to

```
?- owns(Thief,cow,jersey).
?- owns(john,A,midget).
?- owns(john,cow,Breed).
```

3. Specify advantages and disadvantages for each of the variable names in Problem 2.

2.3 FURTHER RESPONSES ("OR")

When Prolog returns a constant name in response to a question with a variable, it pauses, waiting for the questioner to signal (by keying in a "return") that the answer is accepted. Instead of just a "return", the questioner may respond with a semicolon (;) followed by the "return". In Prolog, the semicolon means 'OR'. Prolog interprets this as a direction to look further through the database to find another pattern that matches the one in the question.

Consider a base that consists of facts about a product and the raw material from which it is made. Figure 2.2 shows such a base.

Figure 2.2

Raw Materials and Products

```
made_into(plums,prunes).
made_into(grapes,raisins).
made_into(apples,sauce).
made_into(grapes,wine).
made_into(apples,wine).
made_into(plums,wine).
```

If asked

```
?- made_into(plums,What).
```

Prolog responds

```
What = prunes
```

and pauses. If the questioner responds with a ; Prolog continues

```
What = wine
```

Another ; from the questioner yields

```
no
```

from Prolog. There are only two matches in our database, so asking for a third match causes Prolog to report failure. In a similar manner, the question

```
?- made_into(What,wine).
```

gets the responses

```
What = grapes ;
What = apples ;
What = plums ;
no
```

We have already mentioned that questions can contain more than one variable. Like our example at the end of Section 2.2

```
?- capital(State,City).
```

this question with two variables will match with any fact in the base. Here, however, we will respond with semicolons to get all possible matches.

```
?- made_into(Source,Product).
Source = plums    Product = prunes ;
Source = grapes   Product = raisins ;
Source = apples   Product = sauce ;
Source = grapes   Product = wine ;
Source = apples   Product = wine ;
Source = plums    Product = wine ;
no
```

When Prolog responds to a query, a specific value is given for each of the variables in the query. The order in which values appear within the group (in the case above, a pair) depends on the particular words that programmer has chosen rather than the order in which they appear in the question. In this case, if the query had been

```
?- made_into(Fruit,Product).
```

the pairs would have been shown in this form:

```
Product = prunes   Fruit = plums
yes
```

This difference happens because of Prolog's way of keeping track of the names (called their internal representation). The order in which the pairs of constants appear, however, will be the same.

EXERCISES 2.3

Suppose you have the database

```
do(monday,call_agent).
do(friday,get_tickets).
do(tuesday,get_money).
do(monday,write_home).
do(friday,pack).
do(thursday,study).
do(tuesday,study).
```

1. What will be Prolog's responses to the following questions? (Assume repeated semicolons)

```
?- do(monday,What).
?- do(tuesday,What).
?- do(When,study).
```

2. Assuming repeated semicolons, how many responses will be given to

```
?- do(When,What).
```

2.4 CONJUNCTIONS ("AND")

More complex queries can be made in Prolog by using the conjunction ",", which means "AND". For example, the question

```
?- made_into(What,raisins), made_into(What,wine).
```

asks "what thing is there that raisins are made of and wine is also made of?" A variable name within the question (between the **?** and the **.**) can only represent one object name at a time. That is, when a variable appears more than once in a question, the only matches that can be made will have the same constant name in every place where that variable name appears. Thus Prolog will answer

```
What = grapes
```

and if the questioner responds with a semicolon and return Prolog will respond

```
no
```

as there are no more successful matches to the complete question. Even though part (the second part) has some matches in the database, no others match both parts. If, however, the question asked is

```
?- made_into(What,raisins), made_into(Else,wine).
```

Prolog responds

```
What = grapes   Else = grapes ;
What = grapes   Else = apples ;
What = grapes   Else = plums ;
no
```

as the questioner provides the semicolons. Prolog has made multiple matches and reported the constants for each variable each time. This is possible because What and Else are two separate variables in this question. They may be matched to the same constant, but do not have to be.

More interesting is a database with several different predicates. If we add some facts about colors to our world (Figure 2.3) we can ask "What red things can be made into wine"?

```
?- made_into(Thing,wine), color(red,Thing).
```

and be told

```
Thing = grapes ;
Thing = apples ;
no
```

or

```
?- made_into(Thing,Product), color(red,Product).
Thing = grapes   Product = wine ;
Thing = apples   Product = wine ;
no
```

Figure 2.3

Raw Materials, Products and Colors

```
made_into(plums,prunes).
made_into(grapes,raisins).
made_into(apples,sauce).
made_into(grapes,wine).
made_into(apples,wine).
made_into(plums,wine).
color(red,grapes).
color(white,grapes).
color(purple,plums).
color(red,apples).
color(red,wine).
color(white,wine).
```

Advanced Variable Uses

There are two uses of variables that do not follow the straightforward idea of the variable that we have discussed so far. These are uses that, while not important to the Prolog we have seen up to this point, will be very useful for more sophisticated programs.

Prolog has a special variable name, the underscore "_", which can be read "don't care". It is used mainly as a place holder and can match any constant, any time. Given the question

```
?- made_into(_,prunes).
```

Prolog will respond

```
yes
```

that prunes are made of something, according to the knowledge contained in the database. The variable _ is not associated with a specific name, so it is anonymous. A constant is the name of a specific object. A variable can represent a number of constants, but only represents one at any one time. In a question, the variable represents a specifc object and the constant name of that object is reported to the user. The anonymous variable indicates that there is some constant in the fact in the specified position, but that the questioner is not concerned about what object it is. If a question has two anonymous variables, the constants in those places need not be the same as they would be with a non-anonymous variable.

The second variation on use of variables is to use them in facts in the database. When a fact is part of a complex definition, it sometimes needs an object, but not necessarily a specific object, as part of the fact. For example,

```
hidden_in(the_dark,Any_object).
```

is a legal fact according to Prolog syntax rules. Do not be concerned if you cannot see a sensible use for this now; later you will.

EXERCISES 2.4

Suppose you have the database
```
do(monday,call_agent).
do(friday,get_tickets).
do(tuesday,get_money).
do(monday,write_home).
do(friday,pack).
do(thursday,study).
do(tuesday,study).
```
1. I want to know what else I have to do on the same day I pack.
   ```
   ?- do(Day,pack), do(Day,Task).
   ```
   What will Prolog say?
2. How can I just ask if I set aside study time, never mind when?
3. How can I find out if I have other things to do on my study days?

SUMMARY

Prolog is a descriptive language, designed to define a knowledge base (usually called a database) and ask questions of that base. Prolog facts are part of the base. Prolog facts are made up of attribute/relationship names followed by object names (arguments). The programmer has responsibility for selecting the form of the facts and understanding the associated meaning. The names of objects in facts are typically constant names, although they can be variables. The attribute/relationship (predicate) names must be constants.

Two types of questions can be asked of a Prolog database. Prolog will answer "yes" or "no" to questions for confirmation of a fact. If Prolog is asked questions with variables, it will return constant names that will create a match between patterns in the question and patterns in the base. A Prolog query can be used both to check for a true instance in the base or to find a constant that specifies a true instance.

Prompting Prolog with a semicolon will cause it to continue a search for more possible matches. Questions can contain a conjunction, with a comma used to join the parts. A variable name stands for one constant at any one time, even if it appears in more than one place in a conjunction.

SYNTAX SUMMARY
Facts
```
predicate(<object1>,<object2>,...).
```

Questions
```
?- predicate(<object1>,<object2>,...).
?- predicate1(<object1.1>,<object1.2>,...),
          predicate2(<object2.2>,...),...
```

constants begin with lower-case letters

variables begin with upper-case letters
    — anonymous variable

, and
; additional answers

EXPERIMENTING WITH CHAPTER 2
Purpose:
    To see: interactive, conversational nature
           entering facts
           asking questions
           consulting files and user

Computers, being general purpose tools, are able to do many things. For a computer to do Prolog, it must have a large set of intructions to tell it how. These instructions (called software) are stored somewhere, either on a disk that you put in the computer or in a permanent storage area in the computer system.

When you are ready to use Prolog on a computer, you (the user) must indicate that intention to the computer, so the system will make the Prolog software available. How you do this will depend on your computer system. For at least one system, you type in

```
> Prolog
```

and the computer responds by printing.

```
Prolog-10   version 3.3
Copyright (C) 1981 by D. Warren, F. Pereira and L. Byrd
| ?-
```

The ?- is the Prolog prompt that tells the user Prolog is "ready and waiting". When you begin, your Prolog database is empty. There are two ways to enter facts into the database. The direct way is to "consult the user" (you). You type in [user]. and the Prolog prompt changes to a bar without the ?-.

```
| ?- [user].
|
```

Prolog is now ready to accept the facts you want to enter. Facts that have typing errors in them may or may not be accepted. Ones with punctuation errors usually will be rejected. When you type an error, you will probably get a message telling you there is a syntax error. If you cannot tell from the messages, you may have to check your system manual to find out what to do to recover from the error.

When you are done entering facts, you must indicate this to Prolog. For many systems, you will key in ˆZ (hold down the control key while you key in either upper or lower case z). Others require a different signal, which should be indicated in your system manual. The ?- prompt will now appear. If you type listing., you will see a list of the facts in your database. If you type a predicate name in parentheses between listing and its period, you will see a list of just that set of predicates.

Another way of building a database for Prolog is to use your computer system's editor to create a file. The editor is another piece of software, not part of Prolog. The Prolog facts can be entered one per line. An advantage to using the editor method is that you can correct typing errors more easily. When you have the facts all entered and leave the editor, you save the file with a name. Now call on Prolog, and in response to the ?- prompt, type the file name in square brackets with a period at the end. Sometimes the file name must be enclosed in single quote marks. This consults the file and puts the facts from the file in the database. For example, if my file is named STAR, the Prolog interaction would look like this.

```
Prolog-10   version 3.3
Copyright (C) 1981 by D. Warren, F. Pereira and L. Byrd
| ?- [star].
star consulted   88 words   0.08 sec.
yes
| ?-
```

You can consult several files, one after another. This will put the files' contents together in the database. Again, you can look at the base by typing "listing." If you want to add more facts you can also consult [user] as above. Prolog systems usually have a mechanism for removing some parts from the database, but this mechanism varies from system to system. Check your system manual for specific instructions.

Now that you have some entries in the database, you are ready to make queries of the base. To ask Prolog a question, you simply type the question after the ?- prompt. Prolog gives you its answer and you respond with a semicolon to find alternative answers or with a return to terminate this question. You can then ask another question to which Prolog again responds. Working in this manner is called *interactive* computer use. The example below shows a complete interaction with Prolog, including building the base and asking questions.

```
Prolog-10   version 3.3
Copyright (C) 1981 by D. Warren, F. Pereira and L. Byrd
| ?- [star].
star consulted   88 words   0.08 sec.
yes
| ?- listing.
```

```
do(monday,call_agent).
do(friday,get_tickets).
do(tuesday,get_money).
do(monday,write_home).
do(friday,pack).
do(thursday,study).
do(tuesday,study).
```

yes

| ?- **do(When,pack)**.

When = friday ;

no

| ?- **[user]**.

| **do(monday,shop)**.
| ^Z

| ?- **listing**.

```
do(monday,call_agent).
do(friday,get_tickets).
do(tuesday,get_money).
do(monday,write_home).
do(friday,pack).
do(thursday,study).
do(tuesday,study).
do(monday,shop).
```

yes
| ?- **do(monday,What**.
** syntax error **
do(monday,What
here
| **do(monday,What)**.

What = call_agent ;
What = write_home ;
What = shop ;

no

| ?- ^Z

```
core    641012 (18944 lo-seg + 4101068 hi-seg)
heap    2048 = 1301 in use + 747 free
global  1451 = 16 in use + 1435 free
local   1024 = 16 in use + 1008 free
trail    511 = 0 in use + 511 free
0.83 sec. runtime
```

These last six lines report some statistics on the amount of computer time and space your Prolog interaction used.

If you want to be able to reuse a database, you want to store it in a file. If you used an editor to build the base, it will still be stored in the original file. If you build or modify the base through [user] you may want to save the active base. Your system may allow it; some Prologs do not. Check your system manual.

When you are done with Prolog, key in ˆZ to indicate you want to stop. Most Prolog systems also create a file, called a log that records the interaction between the user and Prolog. Check your system for a file, perhaps called Prolog.log.

EXERCISES CHAPTER 2

1. Identify the Prolog concept or concepts described by each phrase below.
   a) The part of a fact that shows the relationship.
   b) The mechanism for joining more that one fact in a query.
   c) The mechanism for requesting multiple responses to a query.
   d) The component that can be matched to constants or variables.
   e) How a world is described in Prolog.
   f) The variable that can be read as "don't care".
   g) What Prolog means when it reports a constant for a variable.
   h) How Prolog responds to a query about a fact with no variables.
2. For each statement, find one answer.
   a) In the following Prolog sentence, find the predicate.
      `carpet(Room,beige).`
   b) In the following Prolog sentence, find an argument.
      `carpet(Room,beige).`
   c) In the following Prolog sentence, find a constant.
      `carpet(Room,beige).`
   d) In the following Prolog sentence, find a variable.
      `carpet(Room,beige).`
3. Write Prolog sentences for the following.
   a) A set of facts with the name and birthplace of everyone in your family.
   b) a query to see who was born where.
   c) A query to see if two people were born in the same place.
   d) Additional facts for the database about the month people were born.
   e) Pick a month and write a query to see if anyone was born then.
   f) Pick a town and a month and write a query to see who was born there, then.

Extending the World Definition: Prolog Rules

The purpose of this chapter is to help the learner:
- define and use Prolog rules, including
   simple rules.
   compound rules.
   multiple rules.
   rules based on rules.
- understand and use recursive rules.
- recognize the sources of some problems in using recursion.

3.1 RULES

We use Prolog by asking questions. Facts form the basis for the answers that Prolog gives in response to the questions. Facts are statements that are true in our database, and thus are the fundamental building blocks of the database that describes a world. We can expand the description of the world we have defined by adding *rules* to the database. These rules, which are built on facts, or on other rules and facts, add another dimension to the informational power of Prolog's responses.

A Prolog rule has two parts:

1. a conclusion and
2. the requirements for the conclusion.

The rule specifies that the conclusion will be considered true if the requirements component is found to be true. For Prolog to answer a question based on a rule, it uses the data available in the base that tells it about the requirements component. If all the requirements can be found to be true, then the conclusion is true.

Syntax of Rules

The general form for Prolog rules is

```
<conclusion> :- <requirements>.
```

The conclusion, which is called the *head* of the rule, is followed by :- which is followed by one or more requirements. The part after the :- is called the *body* of the rule. The :- can usually be read as "if." A fact is actually a rule with no body.

Syntax Rules: Rules

- conclusion in head (one predicate)
- requirements in body (zero or more predicates)
- :- between head and body, if any
- period (full stop) at end

As an example of a rule, we might say we can conclude that "the sky is blue today if today's weather outlook is described as fair." In Prolog, the rule in this example could be expressed as

```
sky(blue) :- outlook(fair).
```

Assume we have a database with some facts from today's weather report,

```
outlook(fair).
high(seventies).
low(fifties).
rain(none).
```

to this base we add the rule

```
sky(blue) :- outlook(fair).
```

Now if we ask Prolog

```
?- sky(blue).
```

it will respond

yes

Since we asked about sky(blue), Prolog looked for a matching pattern in the data base. It found the pattern as the head of a rule, the rule that the sky is blue if the outlook is fair. Prolog then had to establish the truth of the items in the body. In this case, it found the fact that the outlook is fair. Prolog concluded from this fact, through the rule we have given it, that the sky is blue. Note that Prolog, having found the rule and discovered that there is a body containing requirements, goes back to the beginning of the database to begin searching for the facts to satisfy the requirements.

The structure of a Prolog rule allows us to specify a conclusion in the head that depends on the requirements indicated in the body. A fact is a rule with no requirement component, so it is a conclusion that is always true.

EXERCISES 3.1

1. Using the above database about weather plus the rule
     ```
     need(umbrella) :- rain(heavy).
     ```
   What will Prolog respond to
     ```
     ?- need(umbrella).
     ```
2. Write a rule that indicates one may wear shorts if the high is in the seventies.
3. Write a rule that says to plan a picnic if there is no rain.

3.2 RULES WITH VARIABLES

While the previous rule is interesting, it might be more useful to define a rule that made reference to a specific day. With this kind of rule, we could generalize over a number of days' weather. For example,

```
color(sky,blue,Day) :- weather(Day,fair).
```
      constants   variable   constant

Within this rule, there are constants and variables. The variable, Day, allows the rule to be applied to more than one instance of fair weather. The constants show the specifics of the rule, that fair weather means a blue sky. The variable stands for one single day throughout the rule. That is, fair weather Monday tells us about Monday's sky color only, not any other day's. In Prolog, this is indicated by the use of the same variable name in both the conclusion and the requirements of the rule. The variable in the rule can refer to different days at different times, but it will refer to only one day at any one time.

A base about this week's weather might include

```
weather(sunday,fair).
weather(monday,overcast).
weather(tuesday,fair).
weather(wednesday,fair).
weather(thursday,overcast).
weather(friday,rainy).
weather(saturday,overcast).
color(sky,blue,Day) :- weather(Day,fair).
```

The rule with variables is part of the database along with the facts.

Now if we ask

```
?- color(sky,blue,Day).
```

Prolog will respond (with our entering the semicolons and returns)

```
Day = sunday ;
Day = tuesday ;
Day = wednesday ;
no
```

We have written our query using Day for the variable. Prolog will not confuse our use of Day as the variable name in the question with our use of the same word in the rule. The word Day in our query is not the same as the word Day in the rule from Prolog's point of view. A variable is considered the same for all appearances in one Prolog sentence, up to the period at the end. A sentence is also known as a *clause*; facts and rules are both clauses, and so are queries. A variable must be associated with the same constant throughout a clause but only within that clause. This is called the *scope* of the variable.

Because of their scope, Day in the rule and Day in the query are different to Prolog. They happen to appear in the same position in a matching predicate, but it is the position instead of the word that is important. We could use another variable instead. Prolog has its own internal representation for the variables in rules so that we are free to use any variable we choose in questions. For example, we might choose When.

```
?- color(sky,blue,When).
When = sunday ;
When = tuesday ;
When = wednesday ;
no
```

If we add another rule to our base which says

```
color(sky,grey,Day) :- weather(Day,overcast).
```

and ask a more general question

```
?- color(sky,Which,When).
```

Prolog will tell us.

```
When = sunday      Which = blue ;
When = tuesday     Which = blue ;
When = wednesday   Which = blue ;
When = monday      Which = grey ;
When = thursday    Which = grey ;
When = saturday    Which = grey ;
no
```

Notice that Prolog came to the blue-sky rule first and reported all the days with blue sky before moving on to the grey-sky days. Even though we used Day as the variable in both rules, the two rules are separate and there is no association between them.

One thing Prolog cannot do is work from conclusions back to requirements. The rule is not symmetric. For example, if we add the fact

```
color(sky.blue.christmas)
```

then ask

```
?- weather(christmas.fair).
```

Prolog will answer

```
no
```

To help understand this directionality, think of the :- as an arrow pointing to the left and the arrow pointing from the requirements to the conclusion. The reason underlying this asymmetry is that Prolog rules mean

conclusion "if" requirements

not

conclusion "if and only if" requirements

Thus

```
happy(jean) :- day(christmas).
```

means "Jean will be happy if it is Christmas" not "Jean will be happy only if it is Christmas" or "It must be Christmas if Jean is happy".

■ EXERCISES 3.2

1. If we added a rule to our weather database
   ```
   bask(sun,When) :- weather(When,fair)
   ```
   and ask
   ```
   ?- bask(sun,Day).
   ```
   how will Prolog respond?
2. Write a rule that says to take an umbrella on a rainy day.
3. Write a rule that says to take an umbrella on an overcast day.

3.3 RULES WITH CONJUNCTIONS

Usually, our rules are designed for conclusions contingent on more than one requirement. To specify more than one requirement, we list them in the right hand part of the rule, with commas (,) between them. The comma can be read "and" just as it was with questions in Chapter 2. Thus, for example,

```
happy(birders,Day) :- weather(Day,fair), active(birds,Day).
```

could be read "Birders are happy on a day if the weather that day is fair and birds are active that day."

If we use our database from above and add this rule about birders being happy, we will have the database:

```
weather(sunday,fair).
weather(monday,overcast).
weather(tuesday,fair).
weather(wednesday,fair).
weather(thursday,overcast).
weather(friday,rainy).
weather(saturday,overcast).
color(sky,blue,Day) :- weather(Day,fair).
color(sky,grey,Day) :- weather(Day,overcast).
happy(birders,Day) :- weather(Day,fair), active(birds,Day).
```

If we now ask

```
?- happy(birders,Day).
```

Prolog will respond

```
no
```

This happens because Prolog has only enough data in its database to find out about one part of the requirements specification. There are facts about weather but none about birds being active. Prolog could not make the conclusion because it could not confirm both parts of the specified requirements. If we add

```
active(birds,sunday).
active(birds,tuesday).
active(birds,thursday).
```

then ask

```
?- happy(birders,When).
```

Prolog tells us

```
When = sunday ;
When = tuesday ;
no
```

Notice that Prolog only reports days when both parts of the requirements component can be confirmed with the variable representing the same specific day (see Figure 3.1). According to our rules, even though the birds were active Thursday, Thursday's overcast weather prevented birders from being happy.

Figure 3.1

Weather and Birding

```
weather(sunday,fair).
weather(monday,overcast).
weather(tuesday,fair).
weather(wednesday,fair).
weather(thursday,overcast).
weather(friday,rainy).
weather(saturday,overcast).
color(sky,blue,Day) :- weather(Day,fair).
color(sky,grey,Day)  :- weather(Day,overcast).
happy(birders,Day)  :- weather(Day,fair), active(birds,Day).
active(birds,sunday).
active(birds,tuesday).
active(birds,thursday).
```

When you as a programmer are writing the Prolog form of a rule you are defining, you may have trouble deciding how many variables to use and where to put them. For many people, it is easier to develop the correct clause if they focus on how they would *confirm* that a constant meets the rule than if they focus their thinking on how to *generate* the constants they want. Instead of thinking about getting information out of the database, think about an individual or an object and list the specifications that must be true in the database about that individual or object. After the rule is written, be sure that the form of the requirements in the body of a rule matches the form of the facts in the database.

▰ EXERCISES 3.3

1. Write a rule that says birders will have mixed feelings about a day when it is rainy and birds are active.
2. According to our base, when will this happen?

3.4 RULES BASED ON OTHER RULES

The requirements in a rule need not only be facts; they can also be conclusions from other rules. For example

```
skyeyes(Person,Day) :- color(sky,Hue,Day),
                       color(eyes,Hue,Person).
```

would allow us to ask whose eyes matched the sky some day this week. It would only work if our earlier database (Figure 3.1) were augmented with some facts about the color of some people's eyes.

For example

```
color(eyes,grey,sue).
```

Three pairs of days and "sue" would be reported in response to

```
?- skyeyes(Who,When).
Who = sue   When = monday ;
Who = sue   When = thursday ;
Who = sue   When = saturday ;
no
```

In this particular example, the variable, Hue, appears only in the requirements component and not in the conclusion component. Nonetheless, Hue is involved in the matching needed to follow this rule. We will return to this example in Chapter 4 when we discuss the way Prolog follows its pattern-matching path through these rules.

In this rule notice that the second part of the body is shown on the next line. Prolog clauses can be spread out like this because it is the period that signals the end of the clause, not the end of a line. The clause may be broken up wherever a space is appropriate. Different layouts are chosen partly due to the size of the rules and partly due to programmer preference. Easy readability should be the main goal in choosing layout.

Multiple Rules

In addition to complex rules that use "and" in the requirements component, rules can use "or" (;) to specify more than one possible set of requirements for a single conclusion. For this circumstance, however, there is a better solution. In our database, we can have more than one rule that yields the same conclusion. These multiple rules will have the same predicate in their heads but different bodies. Say we use our database about weather and birders, add facts

```
observed(rarebird,wednesday).
observed(rarebird,friday).
```

and add the rule

```
happy(birders,Day) :- observed(rarebird,Day).
```

Our complete database is now

```
weather(sunday,fair).
weather(monday,overcast).
weather(tuesday,fair).
weather(wednesday,fair).
weather(thursday,overcast).
weather(friday,rainy).
weather(saturday,overcast).
color(sky,blue,Day) :- weather(Day,fair).
color(sky,grey,Day) :- weather(Day,overcast).
happy(birders,Day) :- weather(Day,fair), active(birds,Day).
happy(birders,Day) :- observed(rarebird,Day).
active(birds,sunday).
active(birds,tuesday).
active(birds,thursday).
observed(rarebird,wednesday).
observed(rarebird,friday).
```

Now we have two ways to conclude that birders will be happy. If we ask

```
?- happy(birders,When).
When = sunday ;
When = tuesday ;
When = wednesday ;
When = friday ;
no
```

The first two days were reported by using the first rule; the second two by using the second rule. If we add another fact,

```
observed(rarebird,tuesday).
```

and ask our question again

```
?- happy(birders,When).
When = sunday ;
When = tuesday ;
When = wednesday ;
When = friday ;
When = tuesday ;
no
```

We have Tuesday reported to us twice, once by each of the two rules. There are two sets of requirements that both lead to the same conclusion. Prolog, following its top to bottom order, first found the rule about active birds and reported each day that met that requirement. Next, Prolog found the rarebird rule and reported days contingent on that. Tuesday met the requirements both times.

If two predicates have the same name but different arity, Prolog treats them as entirely different rules.

```
a_name(Part1,Part2) :-
a_name(Thing) :- ......
```

These two rules are not seen as similar by Prolog. Anytime that a rule is used, the shape of the components must match. Thus, the variation in the arity makes a match to both rules impossible.

EXERCISES 3.4

Suppose you had a database:
```
        married(ann,abe).
        mother(ann,bet)
        mother(ann,cat).
        father(Man,Child) :- married(Woman,Man),
                             mother(Woman,Child).
        parent(Person,Child) :- mother(Person,Child).
        parent(Person,Child) :- father(Person,Child).
```
1. What will be Prolog's response to:
```
        ?- mother(ann,Whom).
        ?- father(abe,Whom).
        ?- parent(Who,bet).
```
2. Write queries to find out
   a) who is married to whom
   b) who has two parents known to the database

3.5 RECURSION

In addition to having rules that use other rules as part of their requirements, we can have rules that use themselves as part of their requirements. For example, suppose we have an automobile named Bessy that several people have owned.

```
owned(bessy,Person) :- bought(bessy,Person,Seller),
            owned(bessy,Seller).
```

This rule may be read as "A person owns the car, Bessy, if that person bought Bessy from someone and that someone was Bessy's owner." This kind of rule is called *recursive* because the relationship in the conclusion appears again (recurs) in the body of the rule, where the requirements are specified. Recursive rules are useful when a relationship carries from one object to the next and from that object on to another. In this case, ownership of Bessy moves from person to person. Our understanding of ownership passing along is expressed syntactically in the recurrence in the rule.

While the relationship appears both in the head and body of the rule, the objects, at least some of which are represented by variables, are different in the two places. The pattern of the relationship, moving from object to object, is defined by the way the variables in the rule are related. Notice the way the variables Person and Seller appear in different places in the rule above. The people represented by the variables take different roles in different parts of the rule.

A recursive rule is a way of generating a chain of relationships. For a recursive rule to be effective, however, there must be some place in this chain of relationships where the recursion stops. In our example, someone bought Bessy from the manufacturer.

```
owner(bessy,Person) :- bought(bessy,Person,manufacturer).
```

This stopping condition must be answerable in the database like any other rule. It can use other rules or facts, but should not use the recursive rule. Every time a recursive step along the chain is taken, some progress is made toward the stopping condition. In our example, each time we chain from a purchaser to the seller, we are getting closer to the original owner.

To specify a recursive rule for Prolog, we need a multiple rule definition. First we give the rule for the stopping condition and then the recursive rule. Occasionally, there will be more than one stopping condition. In those instances all the stopping rules should be written into the database before the recursive rule. Below is an example database and examples of questions and responses. Later (in Chapter 4) we will consider the process Prolog uses to keep track of the recursion. It is more important now to learn what Prolog does than to investigate the underlying process.

In this base, the first two lines make up the rule for ownership and the last
four lines are facts.

```
owned(bessy,Person) :- bought(bessy,Person,manufacturer).
owned(bessy,Person) :- bought(bessy,Person,Seller),
          owned(bessy,Seller).
bought(bessy,abe,ben).
bought(bessy,ben,carl).
bought(bessy,carl,fred).
bought(bessy,fred,manufacturer).
```

We can inquire about any one of these people owning Bessy.

```
?- owned(bessy,abe).
yes
?- owned(bessy,sam).
no
```

Or we can present the more general question.

```
?- owned(bessy,Who).
Who = fred ;
Who = abe ;
Who = ben ;
Who = carl ;
no
```

Note the order in which these names appeared. Putting the stopping case first
applies to the components of the multiple rule that defines the recursion; it is
not a restriction on the ordering of the facts that the rule will use to reach its
conclusions. The facts above could be in any order. For example,

```
bought(bessy,fred,manufacturer).
bought(bessy,ben,carl).
bought(bessy,abe,ben).
bought(bessy,carl,fred).
```

Whenever we ask for all the owners of Bessy, however, Fred will be reported
first. His ownership is based on the first part of the rule, so it is verified first.
The order in which the others will be reported will depend on their order in
the base, not, say, on the order in which Bessy was acquired. Thus, using the
order of facts in the second case above, the query and the response are

```
?- owned(bessy,Who).
Who = fred ;
Who = ben ;
Who = abe ;
Who = carl ;
no
```

Here is another example with a recursive rule. The example is built on parent/child relationships. Family tree descriptions are some of the most straightforward examples of Prolog recursion. They are common textbook examples because families are full of relationships that move from object (person) to object (person). Again, the non-recursive part of the rule for ancestor is specified before the recursive part of the rule.

```
mother(ann,bet).
mother(ann,cat).
mother(bet,may).
mother(may,nan).
parent(Person,Child) : mother(Person,Child).
ancestor(Person,Other) :- parent(Person,Other).
ancestor(Person,Other) :- parent(Person,Middle),
          ancestor(Middle,Other).

?- ancestor(Older,Younger).

Younger = bet   Older = ann ;
Younger = cat   Older = ann ;
Younger = may   Older = bet ;
Younger = nan   Older = may ;
Younger = may   Older = ann ;
Younger = nan   Older = ann ;
Younger = nan   Older = bet ;
no
```

EXERCISES 3.5

1. Add these three predicates to the database immediately above.
   ```
   married(abe,ann).
   father(Man,Child) :- mother(Woman,Child),
   married(Man,Woman).
   parent(Person,Child) :- father(Person,Child).
   ```
   Now how will Prolog respond to
   ```
   ?- ancestor(Older,Younger).
   ```
2. Sally invented a new game called Glump. She taught it to Joe, who taught it to Sam and May. May taught it to Leo and he, in turn, taught it to his sister. Write a database using a recursive rule that will tell us who knows how to play Glump.

3.6 POTENTIAL PROBLEMS WITH RECURSION

Sometimes in Prolog recursive rules do not result in the behavior we had planned. This misbehavior is not a result of providing the wrong rule; it has to do with the mechanism Prolog uses to try to arrive at conclusions from rules. You can avoid a number of problems by keeping in mind a few pointers for writing recursive rules.

One suggestion has already been discussed: that the stopping case should be written first in the base. Because Prolog starts at the top of the database, putting the stopping case above the recursive rule ensures it will be tried before another step in the recursive chain is generated. When the end of the chain is reached, it will be noted and the recursion will be stopped, not by-passed.

A second suggestion for more effective recursive rules is to put the recurring predicate at the end of the body of the recursive rule rather than at the beginning. This often helps contain the recursion on a narrower path, and sometimes is necessary if queries are going to be answered at all. When a recursive rule has the recurring predicate as the last part of the body of the rule, it is called *tail recursive* and the process, tail recursion.

For example, the recursive rule for ancestor that we used earlier could have been written with the recurring predicate first.

```
ancestor(Person,Other) :- parent(Person,Middle),
                ancestor(Middle,Other).
ancestor(Person,Other) :- ancestor(Middle,Other),
                parent(Person,Middle).
```

Either form will work for some queries. If we have a database using this second form, and make a query about all ancestors, however, the processing of this rule does not terminate correctly.

```
parent(ann,bet).
parent(bet,cat).
ancestor(Person,Other) :- parent(Person,Other).
ancestor(Person,Other) :- ancestor(Middle,Other),
                parent(Person,Middle).
?- ancestor(Older,Younger).
Older = ann   Younger = bet ;
Older = bet   Younger = cat ;
Older = ann   Younger = cat ;
[ Out of space ]
[ Execution aborted ]
?-
```

After the three correct answers, Prolog went into an endless circle between the two ancestor predicates in the recursive rule. The check for a parent fact is not inside the circle, so it could not indicate the stop. Before long, the space available in the computer was filled up with Prolog's records of the circles. At that point, the Prolog system refused to look further and stopped the execution.

Recursive rules that are written contrary to one or both of these two suggestions may still work correctly, at least for some kinds of queries. A request for all the values that a variable can take (for example, ?- owned(bessy,Who).) is more apt to create a problem than a more specific request (for example, ?-owned(bessy,abe).) The Prolog user needs to choose the way rules are written so that they match expected use of the rules.

Another potential source of problems with recursion can occur when the user did not mean to use recursion at all. If one rule has in its requirements the conclusion of a second rule, while the second rule has the conclusion of the first rule in its requirements, an oscillating recursion can be set up. For example,

```
brother(joe,ann).
brother(He,She) :- sister(She,He).
sister(She,He) :- brother(He,She).
?- sister(ann,Who).
Who = joe ;
Who = joe ;
Who = joe ;
Who = joe
?-
```

This base and request set up a cycle of rule calling upon rule that is fundamentally recursion, although it was not intended. The source of the problem in the base above is quite evident: brother is defined in terms of sister; sister is defined in terms of brother. In a larger, more complex world description where more than two definitions are involved in the cycle, it could be more difficult to discover.

The person defining rules should remain alert to the potential problems with recursion. There is always the possibility of the rules continuing to generate patterns that will not reach the stopping case. Continued generation of patterns like this is called infinite recursion. Programmers sometimes use infinite recursion on purpose but usually it appears by accident.

Recursion, however, provides a useful and powerful way of writing rules. Prolog programmers use it regularly in describing the world in their Prolog database. In order to make writing recursive rules easier, recall the earlier discussion about writing any rule: it is often easier to write the rules if you focus on the way you would confirm that an object follows the rule than if you focus on trying to generate objects to meet the rule. Additionally, for writing recursive rules, use a two-step process. First, write the rule so that it is a correct definition, and then think about rearranging components to get them in the best order.

EXERCISES 3.6

1. Here is an earlier base with some rules added. Prolog will not answer the query correctly. Why?

```
married(ann,abe).
mother(ann,bet).
mother(ann,cat).
mother(Woman,Child) :- father(Man,Child),
          married(Woman,Man).
father(Man,Child) :- mother(Woman,Child),
          married(Woman,Man).
parent(Person,Child) :- mother(Person,Child).
parent(Person,Child) :- father(Person,Child).
?- mother(ann,Whom).
```

2. What is a potential problem with this rule and how should it be corrected?

```
do(First_half,Second_half) :-
          do(First_quarter,Second_half),
          check(First_half,First_quarter).
```

SUMMARY

Rules can be added to facts in a database. The conclusion of a rule is in the rule's head and the requirements for the conclusion are in the rule's body. Rules can have constants and variables. The body of a rule may include a conjunction and may include the conclusion of another rule as part of its requirements. There may be more than one rule that specifies the same conclusion. In the case of recursion, there will usually be one that specifies the stopping case and one that gives the recursive rule. Careful choice and ordering of components in the body of the recursive rule, along with putting the stopping case first, will help guarantee that recursive rules behave as desired.

SYNTAX SUMMARY
Rules

```
<conclusion> :- <requirement1>,
          <requirement2>,..,<requirementN>.
```

EXPERIMENTING WITH CHAPTER 3
Purpose:
   To see: adding rules to a base
           making queries based on rules
           interrupting processing

Rules are added to the database using the same mechanism as is used with facts, either through consulting [user] or consulting a file that has been created with the system's editor.

When you do listing, you may find that Prolog has replaced the variable names in your rules with another kind of name. Prolog also may arrange the rules with different spacing from the way you wrote them, but it will not rearrange the order of the predicates in the body of the rule. Prolog groups like predicates together, but within the group, it maintains the order in which the predicates were entered.

By the time you are using rules, you may find you want to tell Prolog to stop what it is doing. This is particularly important if Prolog seems to be doing nothing for longer than the time it normally takes to respond. The process may have gone into an uncontrolled recursion. Telling Prolog to stop is called an *interrupt*. Check your system manual to find out how this is done. On some systems, a ˆC (CONTROL C) interrupts Prolog and presents the user with some choices about what to do next.

EXERCISES CHAPTER 3

1. Identify the Prolog concept or concepts described by each phrase below.
    a) The contents of a Prolog database.
    b) The two parts of a Prolog rule.
    c) The part of a rule containing the requirements component.
    d) When Prolog uses a rule, the first part that will be matched.
    e) The two ways objects can be represented in rules.
    f) The number of predicates in the head of a rule and the number in the body.
    g) Rules in which the predicate from the conclusion also appears in the requirements.
    h) The two parts that are almost always included in a recursive rule.
2. Using the Prolog database given below, select the number in front of the line or lines that show an example of the terms below.
    ```
    [1] knows(sally) :- knows(joe).
    [2] knows(Hearer) :- tells(Hearer,Teller), knows(Teller).
    [3] tells(sue,sally).
    [4] knows(joe).
    ```
    a) fact
    b) compound rule
    c) multiple rule
    d) recursive rule
    e) stopping case
    f) recursive case
3. Write Prolog databases to describe these situations.
    a) Shop at the grocery store that has the best vegetables.
    b) Shop at the market that has the lowest price on turkey.
    c) Shop at a store if it has good vegetables and beef on special.
    d) Shop at Ben's market.
    e) Four students saw the note Tom wrote to Joe. They sit in a row in class: Tom, Mary, Sally, Joe. Each one looked at the note before passing it on.

Prolog Processing

The purpose of this chapter is to help the learner:
- understand the sequence of steps Prolog uses to respond to a question.
- recognize which variables will be instantiated and in what order.
- define the scope of a variable.
- follow the pattern of Prolog's backtracking.

4.1 PROCESS

Up to this point, we have been focusing on *what* Prolog does. We have discussed the interaction between Prolog and the person using Prolog, observing the behavior that Prolog displays to the user. We have, however, briefly mentioned *how* Prolog does what it does. Prolog's processing was implied in our use of the term "pattern matching," and in noting that Prolog "goes to the top of the database" to begin a search for a fact or rule. Additionally, order in processing is implied by the recommendation to always have the stopping case for a recursion come "before" the recursive rule in the database. In this chapter, we will discuss these matters and some others that are affected by *how* Prolog does its work.

It is important to recognize that "what Prolog does" and "how Prolog does it" are two different ways to look at Prolog's processing (or any other processing, for that matter). Our fundamental goal is always to get Prolog to do what we want; in using Prolog, our primary focus is always on that "what." In many cases, however, our knowing how Prolog is doing its work will help us to build our database in a way that makes Prolog more effective and efficient. Additionally, something may go wrong so that Prolog does not behave as we want. Knowing some of the process Prolog is using may help us discover the reason for the problem.

Matching Facts and Questions

In its simplest form, a Prolog database consists of only facts. Recall that the general form of a fact is a predicate followed by one or more arguments in parentheses. In our simplest interaction, we present Prolog with a question that asks whether a fact is in the database. For example,

```
weather(sunday,fair).
weather(monday,overcast).
weather(tuesday,fair).
weather(wednesday,fair).
weather(thursday,overcast).
weather(friday,rainy).
weather(saturday,overcast).

?- weather(friday,rainy).
```

Prolog's task is to find the fact that matches the question. Prolog begins at the top of the database (first fact entered), trying to match the predicate in the question with the predicate in the fact. It moves down the list of facts until it finds a matching predicate. Next, it checks all the arguments of the predicate to see if the ones in the question match with the ones in the fact. If all the arguments match, Prolog reports

yes

If, however, all the arguments in this fact do not match those in the question, Prolog continues its search. It goes to the next fact and tries again to find a predicate and a complete match. If it reaches the end of the base without finding a match, Prolog reports

no

Observing this process, we are reminded that a "no" response from Prolog means only that data in this base does not indicate a "yes" answer.

━━ **EXERCISES 4.1**

1. How many different facts can be matched in the database we were working with above?
2. If we add a fact to the database
   ```
   weather(friday,fair).
   ```
   so that we have two facts of the form
   ```
   weather(friday,<some>).
   ```
   how will Prolog treat this duplication

4.2 QUESTIONS WITH VARIABLES

When we use a variable, we are using a special name to stand in place of a specific object as an argument in a predicate. The name of the specific object is constant while the variable can name various objects. The variable name can stand for only one constant at a time.

To understand how Prolog uses variables, we have to differentiate between variables that have been associated with a specific constant name and ones that are in an unattached state, not currently associated with any one specific constant name. These two conditions are called

instantiated: the variable is associated with one specific constant name of an object.

uninstantiated: the variable is not currently associated with any specific constant name of an object.

The process of associating a variable with a specific constant is called instantiation of the variable.

Say we have a database of facts and ask a question with a variable name as an argument of the predicate.

```
?- weather(When,overcast).
```

Prolog begins trying to match the predicate from the top of the database just as it did with a predicate with no variables. When it finds a fact with a matching predicate, Prolog checks for a match in the arguments. If all constant arguments match and the number of arguments matches, Prolog instantiates the variable to the constant found in the corresponding position in the fact. The variable is instantiated with the constant that is the argument in the fact. Prolog then reports that instantiation to the user.

```
When = monday
```

Prolog is reporting that the answer to the question is "yes" if the variable is associated with the particular constant. At this point, we may simply accept this answer by keying in a return. If we key in a return, the questioning is complete and Prolog returns to the prompt, **?-**.

Frequently, however, we key in a semicolon, meaning "or." This asks Prolog to continue its search for another fact that matches the question as stated. Prolog now uninstantiates the variable from the first constant and moves on down the database, looking for another match. This process of uninstantiating and looking further is called *backtracking*. It is called backtracking because Prolog "steps back" from an instatiation point to look for another possibility. Imagine that you need to close all the windows in a house like this one.

Figure 4.1

Backtracking in a House

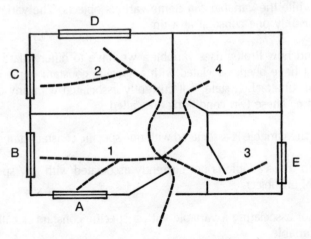

You go in the outside door, decide to close the windows in room 1, close window A, close window B, choose room 2, close window D, close window C, choose room 4, choose room 3, close window E. Every time you back up to a decision point and move on to another choice of a window or a room, you are backtracking.

In processing a question, Prolog uses this kind of pattern. It continues backtracking and instantiating the variable, making as many matches as it can, as long as we keep prompting it with semicolons.

```
When = monday ;
When = thursday ;
When = saturday ;
no
```

Prolog reported "no" when it reached the end of the base, telling us there are no more matches available. When Prolog finishes a searching cycle and returns to the prompt **?-**, all variables are uninstantiated. In fact, the variable name from the just-completed question no longer exists with any meaning to Prolog. This is the case whether we forced Prolog to work through all possibilities or just accepted the first one.

■ **EXERCISES 4.2**

1. How many constants will be reported to
   ```
   ?- weather(When,fair).
   ```
2. What will be the response to
   ```
   ?- weather(friday,Outlook).
   ```

4.3 QUESTIONS WITH MULTIPLE VARIABLES

The question we ask of Prolog may have more than one variable. In this case, Prolog begins on its pattern matching task and follows the same process, instantiating all the variables in the specified question whenever it can match a fact. The instantiations are reported for each match.

```
?- weather(When,What).
```

```
When = sunday      What = fair ;
When = monday      What = overcast ;
When = tuesday     What = fair ;
When = wednesday   What = fair ;
When = thursday    What = overcast ;
When = friday      What = rainy ;
When = saturday    What = overcast ;
```

```
no
```

Questions with Conjunctions

The questions we have looked at so far only contain one predicate. Prolog uses the same pattern matching process when presented with a question that contains a conjunction of predicates, such as

```
made_into(What,prunes),made_into(What,wine).
```

Here we are asking Prolog to instantiate the variable, What, to a constant so that facts can be found that match both parts of the question.

Prolog matches the predicates left to right. It begins by treating the first predicate and its arguments as if it were a simple question. It looks through the database until it finds a matching fact and instantiates its variable or variables. Then it looks at the next predicate in the question. Any variable that was instantiated in the first match will have that value when the second match is started.

Now Prolog begins at the top of the database, treating this second predicate as an independent pattern to match, but with the instantiated variables treated as constants. Prolog looks through the base, seeking a pattern that matches the second predicate. If it finds a match, instantiation is extended into these variables. This process continues through as many cycles as are needed to match all the parts of the question.

When Prolog can completely match all parts of the conjunction, it reports the instantiations. If we prompt Prolog with a semicolon at this point, it will go on to try to make other matches using backtracking. First, Prolog uninstantiates the variables in the match that was done last. In a compound question, this will be the component farthest to the right. Prolog maintains the next-to-the-last instantiation and moves down through the database, looking for another match for the rightmost component, searching and matching to the bottom of the base. When potential matches for the last predicate are exhausted, Prolog steps back to the second-from-the-right component of the question and uninstantiates the variables there. Then it searches down the base, repeating the search, match and instantiate pattern.

Below is an example, which, for simplicity's sake, has only two components in the conjunction in the question. The process is the same for more components. The lines in the database are numbered for reference in the process. In the extended description that follows, the indentation pattern shows the left-to-right and back-to-left processing of the components of the question.

```
 1.  shade(sox,black).
 2.  shade(sox,red).
 3.  shade(sox,green).
 4.  shade(sox,white).
 5.  color(shoes,black).
 6.  color(shoes,white).
 7.  color(sneakers,red).
 8.  color(skates,white).
 9.  color(running_shoes,black).
10.  color(boots,brown).
```

What footgear can I wear so that the shade of my sox matches the color of my footgear?

```
?- shade(sox,Hue), color(Footgear,Hue).

Hue = black   Footgear = shoes ;
Hue = black   Footgear = running_shoes ;
Hue = red     Footgear = sneakers ;
Hue = white   Footgear = shoes ;
Hue = white   Footgear = skates ;
no
```

Searching from the top, shade(sox,Hue) matches shade(sox,black) line 1
    Hue is instantiated to black.
    color(Footgear,Hue) becomes color(Footgear,black) for search.

        Searching from the top for match to color(Footgear,black),
        color(Footgear,black), matches color(shoes,black) line 5
        Hue = black Footgear = shoes reported, given ;
        Footgear uninstantiated, search continues at line 6
        color(Footgear,black) matches color(running__shoes,black) line 9
        Hue = black Footgear = running__shoes reported, given ;

    Footgear uninstantiated, search continues at line 10
    No more matches to color(Footgear,black), so backtrack.

Prolog steps back to the next component to the left
Hue is uninstantiated, search continues at line 2
Search is for a new match to shade(sox,Hue)
shade(sox,Hue) matches shade(sox,red) in line 2

    Hue is instantiated to red.
    color(Footgear,Hue) becomes color(Footgear,red) for search.

        Searching from the top for match to color (Footgear,red),
        color(Footgear,red) matches color(sneakers,red) line 7
        Hue = red Footgear = sneakers reported, given ;

    Footgear uninstantiated, search continues at line 8
    No more matches to color(Footgear,red), so backtrack.

Prolog steps back to the next component to the left.
Hue uninstantiated, search continues at line 3
Search is for a new match to shade(sox,Hue)
shade(sox,Hue) matches shade(sox,green) in line 3

    Hue is instantiated to green
    color(Footgear,Hue) becomes color(Footgear,green)
    Search is from the top for match to color(Footgear,green),
    No match is found for color(Footgear,green), so backtrack.

Prolog steps back to the next component to the left.
Hue is uninstantiated
Search is for a new match for shade(sox,Hue) from line 4
shade(sox,Hue) matches shade(sox,white) in line 4

    Hue is instantiated to white
    color(Footgear,Hue) becomes color(Footgear,white)
    Search begins at the top for match to color(Footgear,white),

        color(Footgear,white) matches color(shoes,white) in line 6
        Hue = white Footgear = shoes reported, given ;

Footgear is uninstantiated
Search for color(Footgear,white) continues at line 7

color(Footgear,white) matches color(skates,white) in line 8
Hue = white   Footgear = skates   reported, given ;

Footgear is uninstantiated
Search for color(Footgear,white) continues at line 9
No more matches for color(Footgear,white) available, so backtrack.

Prolog steps back to the next component to the left.
Hue is uninstantiated
Search for new match to shade(sox,Hue) begins at line 5
No more matches for shade(sox,Hue) available, so backtrack.
No further components to the left, so Prolog reports "no"

Notice that all the shade predicates came before the color predicates and in the question, the shade component came before the color component. This is not necessary; they could appear in either order. The order in both the base and the question will, however, affect the order of the responses.

▓ EXERCISES 4.3

1. Given the database above, what responses (in what order) would Prolog give to
   ```
   ?- color(Footgear,Hue), shade(sox,Hue).
   ```
2. If the base had been written using color as the predicate throughout (make shade into color) and asked
   ```
   ?- color(sox,Hue), color(Footgear,Hue).
   ```
   how would Prolog's answers be different, and why?

4.4 SCOPE OF VARIABLES

In a question with a conjunction, we usually have the same variable name in more than one place. When we are given an answer, that variable will be instantiated to the same constant throughout all parts of the question. The group of predicates where a variable name indicates the sharing of an instantiation is the *scope* of the variable. In the context of questions, the scope is from the prompt to the period at the end of the question.

When we ask another question, the instantiations will not carry over, even if we are using the same variable name. Prolog has effectively forgotten the variable name. The scope of a variable cannot include separate questions. If we want to include more predicates in a variable's scope, we must combine all predicates in one question. In fact, this is why we use questions that contain conjunctions. Questions with just one predicate can give us only bottom-level answers when our database is made only of facts.

Rules

Questions using conjunctions become complex and tedious to ask. Even keying them in without typing errors is a problem. Using rules simplifies this situation. A rule is a definition that allows us to name one predicate in a question in place of a complex conjunction of simple predicates.

It is not surprising, then, to find that Prolog treats rules very much like questions with conjunctions. When the pattern to be matched turns out to be a rule, the body of the rule is handled like a question. The variables in the head of the rule are instantiated to the same constants as the corresponding variables in the body. In rules, the scope of a variable includes all appearances in the head and the body within the rule. The following examples, which all use the database in Figure 4.2, show instantiation response patterns for rules, simple to complex. The lines in the database are numbered for reference.

Figure 4.2

Rules Using Weather

```
 (1)  weather(sunday,fair)*
 (2)  weather(monday,overcast).
 (3)  weather(tuesday,fair).
 (4)  weather(wednesday,fair).
 (5)  weather(thursday,overcast).
 (6)  weather(friday,rainy).
 (7)  weather(saturday,overcast).
 (8)  color(sky,blue,Day) :- weather(Day,fair).
 (9)  color(sky,grey,Day) :- weather(Day,overcast).
(10)  color(eyes,grey,sue).
(11)  plan(picnic,sunday) :- weather(sunday,fair).
(12)  ambivalent(birders,Day) :- weather(Day,rainy),
                active(birds,Day).
(13)  skyeyes(Person,Day) :- color(sky,Hue,Day),
                color(eyes,Hue,Person).
(14)  happy(birders,Day) :- weather(Day,fair),
                active(birds,Day).
(15)  happy(birders,Day) :- observed(rarebird,Day).
(16)  active(birds,sunday).
(17)  active(birds,tuesday).
(18)  active(birds,friday).
(19)  observed(rarebird,wednesday).
(20)  observed(rarebird,tuesday).
```

```
?- plan(picnic,sunday).
yes

plan(picnic,sunday).                    found rule line 11
   weather(sunday,fair).                found fact line 1
yes

?- color(sky,blue,tuesday).
yes

color(sky,blue,tuesday).                found rule line 8
   weather(tuesday,fair).               found fact line 3
yes

?- color(sky,blue,When).
When = sunday ;
When = tuesday ;
When = wednesday ;
no

color(sky,blue,When).                   found rule line 8
   weather(When,fair).                  found fact line 1
   weather(sunday,fair).                instantiate When
   When = sunday ;                      semicolon prompt
   weather(When,fair).                  found fact line 3
   weather(tuesday,fair).               instantiate When
   When = tuesday ;                     semicolon prompt
   weather(When,fair).                  found fact line 4
   weather(wednesday,fair).             instantiate When
   When = wednesday ;                   semicolon prompt
   weather(When,fair).                  no more matches
color(sky,blue,When).                   no more matches
no

?- color(sky,Hue,When).
Hue = blue    When = sunday ;
Hue = blue    When = tuesday ;
Hue = blue    When = wednesday ;
Hue = grey    When = monday ;
Hue = grey    When = thursday ;
Hue = grey    When = saturday
no

color(sky,Hue,When).                    found rule line 8
   color(sky,blue,When).                instantiate Hue
      weather(When,fair).               found fact line 1
      weather(sunday,fair).             instantiated When
      Hue = blue    When = sunday ;     semicolon prompt
```

```
        weather(When,fair).                   found fact line 3
        weather(tuesday,fair).                instantiated When
        Hue = blue   When = tuesday ;         semicolon prompt

        weather(When,fair).                   found fact line 4
        weather(wednesday,fair).              instantiated When
        Hue = blue   When = wednesday ;       semicolon prompt

        weather(When,fair).                   no more matches
      color(sky,blue,When).                   no more matches
    color(sky,Hue,When).                      found rule line 9
      color(sky,grey,When).                   instantiate Hue
        weather(When,overcast).               found fact line 2
        weather(monday,overcast).             instantiated When
        Hue = grey   When = monday ;          semicolon prompt

        weather(When,overcast).               found fact line 5
        weather(thursday,overcast).           instantiated When
        Hue = grey   When = thursday ;        semicolon prompt
        weather(When,overcast).               found fact line 7
        weather(saturday,overcast).           instantiated When
        Hue = grey   When = saturday ;        semicolon prompt

        weather(When,overcast).               no more matches
      color(sky,grey,When).                   no more matches
    color(sky,Hue,When).                      no more matches
    no

    ?- ambivalent(birders,When).
    When = friday ;
    no

    ambivalent(birders,When).                 found rule line 12
      weather(When,rainy).                    found fact line 6
      weather(friday,rainy).                  instantiate When
        active(birds,friday).                 found fact line 18
    When = friday ;                           semicolon prompt
      weather(When,rainy).                    no more matches
    ambivalent(birders,When).                 no more matches
    no

    ?- skyeyes(Who,When).
    Who = sue   When = monday ;
    Who = sue   When = thursday ;
    Who = sue   When = saturday ;
    no
```

`skyeyes(Who,When)`	found rule line 13
`  color(sky,Hue,When).`	found rule line 8
`    color(sky,blue,When).`	instantiate Hue
`      weather(When,fair).`	found fact line 1
`      weather(sunday,fair).`	instantiate When
`        color(eyes,blue,Who).`	no matches on second part of 13
`      weather(When,fair).`	uninstantiate When
`      weather(tuesday,fair).`	instantiate When
`        color(eyes,blue,Who).`	no matches on second part of 13
`      weather(When,fair).`	uninstantiate When
`      weather(wednesday,fair).`	instantiate When
`        color(eyes,blue,Who).`	no matches on second part of 13
`      weather(When,fair).`	uninstantiate When
`    color(sky,blue,When).`	no more matches
`  color(sky,Hue,When).`	found rule line 9
`    color(sky,grey,When).`	instantiate Hue
`      weather(When,overcast).`	found fact line 2
`      weather(monday,overcast).`	instantiate When
`        color(eyes,grey,Who).`	found fact line 10 on second part of 13
`      Who = sue   When = monday ;`	semicolon prompt (redo second part of 13)
`        color(eyes,grey,Who).`	no more matches on second part of 13
`      weather(When,overcast).`	found fact line 5 (redo rule in line 9)
`      weather(thursday,overcast)`	instantiate When
`        color(eyes,grey,Who).`	found fact line 10
`      Who = sue   When = thursday ;`	semicolon prompt (redo second part of 13)
`        color(eyes,grey,Who).`	no more matches
`      weather(When,overcast).`	found fact line 7 (redo rule in line 9)
`      weather(saturday,overcast).`	instantiate When
`        color(eyes,grey,Who).`	found fact line 10
`      Who = sue   When = saturday ;`	semicolon prompt (redo second part of 13)
`        color(eyes,grey,Who).`	no more matches
`      weather(When,overcast).`	no more matches
`    color(sky,Hue,When).`	no more matches
`skyeyes(Who,When).`	no more matches
`no`	

1. List the pattern of seeking and matching for the question
    happy(birders,When).
2. How would the pattern of seeking and matching differ if the rule about skyeyes were

    skyeyes(Person,Day) :- color(eyes,Hue,Person),
                           color(sky,Hue,Day).

4.5 RECURSION

Recursion presents a special set of circumstances when we talk about how Prolog is doing its work. In recursion, the same rule is used over and over to work through the chain of relationships, finally reaching the stopping case. The process remains the same, however, with variables being instantiated and new patterns being set up for matching. The following examples use the database in Figure 4.3.

Figure 4.3

Owners of Bessy

```
(1)  owned(bessy,Person) :- bought(bessy,Person,manufacturer).
(2)  owned(bessy,Person) :- bought(bessy,Person,Seller),
                       owned(bessy,Seller).
(3)  bought(bessy,fred,manufacturer).
(4)  bought(bessy,ben,carl).
(5)  bought(bessy,carl,fred).
```

```
?- owned(bessy,fred).
yes
```

owned(bessy,fred).	found rule line 1
bought(bessy,fred,manufacturer)	found fact line 3

```
?- owned(bessy,ben).
yes
```

owned(bessy,ben).	found rule line 1
bought(bessy,ben,manufacturer).	no match
owned(bessy,ben).	found rule line 2
bought(bessy,ben,Seller).	
bought(bessy,ben,carl).	
owned(bessy,carl).	found rule line 1
bought(bessy,carl,manufacturer).	no match

```
        owned(bessy,carl).                              found rule line 2
           bought(bessy,carl,Seller).
           bought(bessy,carl,fred).
              owned(bessy,fred).                         found rule line 1
                 bought(bessy,fred,manufacturer).        match 3
yes
```

Note the separate instantiations of Seller. The scope of Seller in each use of the rule does not overlap the others. In this example, lines marked -redo- show repeated attempts to match a predicate.

```
?- owned(bessy,Who).
Who = fred ;
Who = ben ;
Who = carl ;
no

owned(bessy,Who).
  bought(bessy,Who,manufacturer).
  bought(bessy,fred,manufacturer).
  Who = fred ;

  bought(bessy,Who,manufacturer).        -redo-
owned(bessy,Who).        -redo-
  bought(bessy,Who,Seller).
  bought(bessy,fred,manufacturer).
    owned(bessy,manufacturer).
      bought(bessy,manufacturer,manufacturer).
      bought(bessy,manufacturer,Person).
  bought(bessy,Who,Seller).        -redo-

      bought(bessy,ben,carl).
        owned(bessy,carl).
          bought(bessy,carl,manufacturer).
          bought(bessy,carl,Seller).
            bought(bessy,carl,fred).
              owned(bessy,fred).
                bought(bessy,fred,manufacturer).
Who = ben ;

  bought(bessy,Who,manufacturer).        -redo-
owned(bessy,Who).        -redo-
  bought(bessy,Who,Seller).
  bought(bessy,fred,manufacturer).
    owned(bessy,manufacturer).
    bought(bessy,manufacturer,manufacturer).
    bought(bessy,manufacturer,Person).
  bought(bessy,Who,Seller).
        bought(bessy,carl,fred).
          owned(bessy,fred).
            bought(bessy,fred,manufacturer).
Who = carl ;

  bought(bessy,Who,manufacturer).        -redo-
owned(bessy,Who).        -redo-
  bought(bessy,Who,Seller).
```

EXERCISES 4.5

1. Trace the seek and match process for this base and question to the point where one instantiation is reported.

```
mother(ann,bet).
mother(bet,may).
parent(Person,Child) :- mother(Person,Child).
parent(Person,Child) :- father(Person,Child).
ancestor(Person,Other) :- parent(Person,Other).
ancestor(Person,Other) :- parent(Person,Middle),
          ancestor(Middle,Other).
married(abe,ann).
father(Man,Child) :- mother(Woman,Child),
          married(Man,Woman).
?- ancestor(Older,Younger).
```

2. If these two facts were added to the database

```
mother(ann,cat).
mother(may,nan).
```

What responses in what order would be reported to

```
?- ancestor(Older,Younger).
```

SUMMARY

In addition to learning what Prolog does, we may want to know how Prolog processes the user's requests. Prolog searches through its database, matching predicates and arguments from questions with predicates and arguments in the database. During matching, variables can be instantiated (if they have been matched with constants in the base) or uninstantiated (if they are currently unmatched). A variable's scope is the range over which an instantiation is shared. In Prolog, the scope is restricted to the clause in which the variable occurs. In questions or rules with conjunctions, the processing works left to right, successively matching predicates and instantiating variables. When Prolog is unable to match a predicate or is told to search further, the farthest-right match is undone and the process moves on from the last choice point. The pattern that Prolog uses, called backtracking, allows repeated search through the database for matches.

EXPERIMENTING WITH CHAPTER 4

Purpose:
    To see: how trace is used
               a trace of a recursive rule

Many Prolog systems have the facility for Prolog to keep a record of the search and match patterns. This mechanism may be called the *trace* or *debug* mode. In displaying the trace, uninstantiated variables are shown in the form of their internal representation: an underscore and a number. A Prolog.log with a record of the complete interaction with tracing of the instantiations follows.

```
Prolog-10   version 3.3
Copyright (C) 1981 by D. Warren, F. Pereira and L. Byrd

| ?- [bessy].

bessy consulted   98 words   0.09 sec.

yes
| ?- trace.
Debug mode switched on.

| ?- owned(bessy,carl).
(1) 0 Call : owned(bessy,carl) ?
(2) 1 Call : bought(bessy,carl,manufacturer) ?
(2) 1 Fail : bought(bessy,carl,manufacturer)
(3) 1 Call : bought(bessy,carl,_68) ?
(3) 1 Exit : bought(bessy,carl,fred)
(4) 1 Call : owned(bessy,fred) ?
(5) 2 Call : bought(bessy,fred,manufacturer) ?
(5) 2 Exit : bought(bessy,fred,manufacturer)
(4) 1 Exit : owned(bessy,fred)
(1) 0 Exit : owned(bessy,carl)

yes
| ?- core   64512 (18944 lo-seg + 45568 hi-seg)

heap      2048 = 1313 in use +   735 free
global    1451 =   16 in use + 1435 free
local     1024 =   16 in use + 1008 free
trail      511 =    0 in use +  511 free

0.98 sec. runtime
```

EXERCISES CHAPTER 4 ███████████████

1. Identify the Prolog concept or concepts described by each phrase below.
    a) The description of variables that depends on whether or not they are associated with a constant object.
    b) Stepping backward through a decision point to take a new path.
    c) In questions with conjunctions, the order in which predicates are matched.
    d) The effect on instantiation of a variable that appears more than once in a question with a conjunction.
    e) The range over which a variable refers to the same constant.
    f) The process during which rules are reused but the scope of the variables is separate.
    g) Recursive rules will process repeatedly until they reach this case.

2. Here is a database and three queries. In what order will the attempted matches be made for each question?

```
carpet(green).
chair(red).
chair(green).
pillows(white).
pillows(green).
?- carpet(Color), chair(Color), pillows(Color).
?- pillows(white), carpet(Color), chair(Color).
?- carpet(green), chair(Color).
```

3. Write Prolog programs to provide
   a) A database with facts that describe your favorite books as funny, sad, science fiction and so on. Add rules that describe what to read in a certain mood.
   b) Write queries to get recommendations for reading based on your mood.
   c) Add the last week's weather day by day and a set of rules describing your mood based on weather conditions.
   d) Write queries to find out what to read on which day. If there could be several books appropriate for one day, try to predict the order in which they will appear.

Lists 5

The purpose of this chapter is to help the learner:
- understand the purpose of lists.
- write a Prolog program using a list.
- understand the head/tail notation.
- write list manipulation rules.

5.1 GROUPING

In the world around us, we know about many specific objects. Humans, needing to simplify their thinking load, use an organizational tactic. We categorize a number of objects into a group, based on some characteristic the objects have in common. Then we are able to deal with the group instead of all the individual objects. In Prolog, the list is a similar mechanism. Lists are used to group objects together; then the list can be manipulated as a single object.

In Chapter 3, on rules, we had a database that included data about birders being happy when a rare bird was sighted. The information on bird sightings, however, is more apt to be a specific bird name, such as condor, than just "rarebird." We could write separate rules for each bird species considered rare, but this would be tedious and repetitive.

Lists
A better method in such circumstances is to have a list of the specific objects and to use items from the list when a particular object is needed. Thus, if we had a list of rare birds in a given area and time of year, and someone reported having seen, say, a western meadowlark, we could use Prolog to find out if that would make birders happy.

We know that Prolog will answer our query by using pattern matching, in this case looking for the bird name we have given it. The object we have in our base, however, is a *list* of names. Prolog must be told that the object is a list and that the name we want found is potentially within that list. The specific objects within a list are called *elements*. Thus, we want to provide a way for Prolog to do its matching with the elements of the list, not the list as a whole.

Syntax of Lists
A list in Prolog can be written in square brackets with commas between the list's elements. For example,

```
[condor,whooping_crane,dusky_seaside_sparrow]
```

If we put this into a database with the list as the argument of a predicate,

```
rarebird([condor,whooping_crane,dusky_seaside_sparrow]).
```

then ask

```
?- rarebird(condor)
```

Prolog answers

```
no
```

In fact if we ask

```
?- rarebird(What).
```

Prolog tells us

```
What = [condor,whooping_crane,dusky_seaside_sparrow]
```

That is, the variable What has been instantiated with the whole list as a single object. Since we want to get at the individual elements, we will write rules using a variable for each of the elements of the list. Each rule will specify a pattern with a variable in a specific location in the list. In the positions we are not concerned about, we will put an underscore. The underscore, remember, means "don't care". Thus, to write a rule that says a <u>Bird</u> is <u>noteworthy</u> if that Bird appears in the first position in our rarebird list, we will write

```
noteworthy(Bird) :- rarebird([Bird,_,_]).
```

By the same token, we will write two more rules, specifying that the Bird could appear in the second or third positions.

```
noteworthy(Bird) :- rarebird([_,Bird,_]).
noteworthy(Bird) :- rarebird([_,_,Bird]).
```

These three rules along with our list of the rarebirds lets us ask the question:

```
rarebird([condor,whooping_crane,dusky_seaside_sparrow]).
noteworthy(Bird) :- rarebird([Bird,_,_]).
noteworthy(Bird) :- rarebird([_,Bird,_]).
noteworthy(Bird) :- rarebird([_,_,Bird]).
?- noteworthy(condor).
yes
```

Condor was found as a noteworthy bird through the use of the first of the three rules. If we want to make changes in which birds are noteworthy, we can alter the base by simply changing the one predicate, rarebird, to one with a new list.

```
rarebird([cardinal,bluebird,meadowlark]).
noteworthy(Bird) :- rarebird([Bird,_,_]).
noteworthy(Bird) :- rarebird([_,Bird,_]).
noteworthy(Bird) :- rarebird([_,_,Bird]).
```

This has gained us some flexibility, but not much, over having a separate fact for each bird. But meanwhile, we have added a constraint on our process, that it only handles lists of three birds. If we want to include more birds, we must write more noteworthy rules and alter the ones we have. Besides, the constraint on the number in the list is not helpful; different size lists of birds are going to be needed.

1. Write a Prolog notation for a list of the colors in the rainbow.
2. Write a predicate that has the list above as the argument for "rainbow."
3. Assuming the rainbow predicate is in a database, write a pair of queries that check to see which constant you chose for the seventh color in the rainbow, purple, violet or some other.

5.2 HEAD AND TAIL

We need a way of looking at the list, different from a "row of objects." Instead, we consider a list to be made of two parts; the *head*, which is the first element in the list, and the *tail*, which is a list of the rest of the elements. Note that the head is an element and the tail is a list. Because the tail is a list, it too has a head and tail.

LIST: [cardinal,bluebird,meadowlark]
HEAD: cardinal
TAIL: [bluebird,meadowlark]

LIST: [bluebird,meadowlark]
HEAD: bluebird
TAIL: [meadowlark]

LIST: [meadowlark]
HEAD: meadowlark
TAIL: [ ]

The tail of the third example above is the special list, the *empty list*. It is a list like any other except that it is empty, so it does not have a head or a tail. (In Chapter 3, we discussed rules having a head and a body. The two uses of "head" are coincidental, not to be associated.)

A good model for this way of thinking of a list is a stack of cards, piled one on top of another, in a box so that we cannot see any card except the top one. The top card is the head of the list, and the rest (everything below the head) is the tail.

If we remove the head from our stack of cards, we find ourselves once more with a stack that has a head and tail. The only difference is that our stack has gotten smaller. Repeating the removal of the current head eventually leads us to the bottom of the stack and an empty box. At this time, we must stop the process because the empty box has no head nor tail with which to continue. The head/tail relationship has moved down the stack of cards to a special case, the stopping place. Observe that this is a recursive pattern. To design a general method for accessing elements of lists, we will use recursion. Because the recursion continues as long as is necessary to reach the stopping case, we can use the method on lists of variable size.

First, however, we have to be able to separate the head and tail of a list. Prolog facilitates this with a special pattern for specifying head and tail, using a vertical bar and square brackets. For example,

    [H|T]

Here H is the variable that represents the element that is the head of the list and T represents the list that is the tail of the list. The head and tail can be constants as well as variables. If we have

    rarebird([cardinal,bluebird,meadowlark]).

in our database and ask

    ?- rarebird([H|T]).

Prolog responds

    H = cardinal   T = [bluebird,meadowlark]

EXERCISES 5.2

1. Identify the head and the tail of the following lists.
    [red,orange,yellow]
    [red,orange]
    [red]
    [ ]
2. Given the database
    author([k_wilhelm,juniper_time,fault_lines]).
    author([u_leguin,left_hand_of_darkness]).
   What will be the responses (user prompting with ;'s) to
    ?- author([Head|Tail]).
3. Given a database with author predicates as above, write a query that would cause Prolog to report all author names (head of lists) without reporting the rest of the list.

5.3 MEMBERSHIP IN A LIST
We are now ready to write the rules that will allow us to find out if a particular name is included in a list. First, an element is a member of a list if it is the head of the list. We define this case in a fact with variables.

    member(Element,[Element|_]).

If this not the case, then the element may still be a member if it is in the tail of the list. We define this case in a recursive rule.

```
member(Element,[_|Tail]) :- member(Element,Tail).
```

The match will always be attempted with the head of the list. If no match is found there, the process moves on to the tail, treating it just like the original list, trying to match its head. Following the rule, Prolog now carries out its searching, using Tail as the list in the definition.

This multiple rule definition for membership,

```
member(Element,[Element|_]).
member(Element,[_|Tail]) :- member(Element,Tail).
```

defines a recursive method for finding a specific element. The non-recursive part of the rule appears first, as it did with our earlier recursive rules. Say we make a query

```
?- member(a,[a,b,c]).
```

Prolog will answer "yes" to this query because the element that is the head of the list matches the first argument of the first rule.

```
?- member(a,[b,a,c]).
```

will also be answered "yes" because the second rule calls on the member rule recursively and thus moves down the list to check for a match.

What makes this recursion stop? There are two possibilities:
- the match is found as it was in the examples above, using the first (non-recursive) part of the multiple rule;
- the match is never found because the name is not in the list.

If the name is not an element of the list, the recursion process will consider smaller and smaller lists until all that is left is the empty list, [ ]. Neither of our member rules say what to do with an empty list; it has neither head nor tail, so our rules do not apply. That is, [ ] does not match either [Element|__] or [__|Element]. Since there is no match to the empty list, the search is unsuccessful and the process stops. The way the two stopping cases are expressed in our rules are different. The first case, where the name is found as the head of a list, is written explicitly in the rule as the first, non-recursive part of the definition. The second case, where the empty list is encountered, is implicit in the original specification, because the empty list has no head nor tail.

Note that the recursive process of looking for an element in a list does not actually modify the list in any way. It simply instantiates the variable, here named Tail, to successively smaller lists. The original list acts as the source for the smaller lists, but remains unchanged itself.

Look carefully at the first part of the membership rule.

```
member(Element,[Element|_]).
```

This is the first time we have seen a fact with variables rather than the constants we have previously seen. The fact shows the relationship between an object and the list of which the object is head. The relationship can be generalized over many lists, so a variable is used to stand in place of the object in the relationship, rather than a constant. This relationship is the conclusion of a rule; the requirements for the conclusion are embedded in the special notation for the head of a list, [H|_]. That is, using this notation is part of the definition of the requirements for the relationship.

EXERCISES 5.3

1. Given this database plus the member rules,
    ```
    author([k_wilhelm,juniper_time,fault_lines]).
    author([u_leguin,left_hand_of_darkness]).
    author([l_m_alcott,little_women]).
    ```
    list all the responses to
    ```
    ?- author(List),member(Element,List).
    ```
2. What query will cause each of the lists to be reported as a unit (rather than as elements)?

5.4 USING MEMBERSHIP
To use the member rule and apply it specifically to the list of rare birds, we could use this database and ask questions.

```
noteworthy(Bird) :-member(Bird,
            [condor,whooping_crane,dusky_seaside_sparrow]).
member(Element,[Element|_]).
member(Element,[_|Tail]) :- member(Element,Tail).

?- noteworthy(condor).
yes

?- noteworthy(robin).
no

?- noteworthy(Which).
Which = condor ;
Which = whooping_crane ;
Which = dusky_seaside_sparrow ;
no
```

A second way to build the rule will provide us with more flexibility. Instead of including the bird list in the noteworthy rule, we can use this form:

```
rarebird([condor,whooping_crane,dusky_seaside_sparrow]).
noteworthy(Bird) :- rarebird(List), member(Bird,List).
member(Element,[Element|_]).
member(Element,[_|Tail]) :- member(Element,Tail).
```

When we make the query

```
?- noteworthy(condor).
```

List is instantiated to the whole list in the rarebird predicate and then the membership predicate searches through the list for specific elements. This works as well as the earlier example and is somewhat more flexible, since only the rarebird list would require alteration to make changes. A second rare-bird list could be added to expand the base. Prolog will process the lists as single objects, in order of their appearance in the base.

```
rarebird([condor,whooping_crane,dusky_seaside_sparrow])
rarebird([blue_bird,cardinal]).
noteworthy(Bird) :- rarebird(List), member(Bird,List).
member(Element,[Element|_]).
member(Element,[_|Tail]) :- member(Element,Tail).

?- noteworthy(What).
What = condor ;
What = whooping_crane ;
What = dusky_seaside_sparrow ;
What = blue_bird ;
What = cardinal ;
no
```

There is, however, a risk in this structure whether it has one list or more. The critical condition is in the noteworthy rule. It must contain the predicate that instantiates List first, and then the predicate that checks for membership in the list. If, in the noteworthy rule, we had put the member predicate before the predicate that instantiates the List, some queries would not be processed correctly. The rearranged rule, named not_worthy, is shown in the database below along with the same member rule and one of the rarebird lists.

```
rarebird([condor,whooping_crane,dusky_seaside_sparrow]).
not_worthy(Bird) :- member(Bird,List), rarebird(List).
member(Element,[Element|_]).
member(Element,[_|Tail]) :- member(Element,Tail).

?- not_worthy(condor).
yes
```

In response to a query about a specific bird, Prolog behaves correctly, but if we ask Prolog to specify all the birds that the base considers not__worthy, it goes out of control.

```
?- not_worthy(What).
What = condor ;
What = whooping_crane ;
What = dusky_seaside_sparrow ;
(out of memory space)
[ Execution aborted ]
```

Rather than telling us that there are no more members of the list, Prolog continues looking for others. If we observe Prolog's processing, we will see the pattern being used. In the following description, variables that start with V represent elements and variables that start with T represent the tail of a list. The first part of the description, through the point where condor is reported, is complete. After that point, only the form of the predicate that is to be matched to the rarebird predicate is shown in the example.

```
?- not_worthy(What).
  not_worthy(What) ?
  member(What,List) ?
  member(What,[What|T1])
  rarebird([What|T1]) ?
  rarebird([condor,whooping_crane,dusky_seaside_sparrow])
  not_worthy(condor)

What = condor ;

  rarebird([V2,What|T2]) ?

What = whooping_crane ;

  rarebird([V2,V3,What|T3]) ?

What = dusky_seaside_sparrow ;

  rarebird([V2,V3,V4,What|T4]) ?
  rarebird([V2,V3,V4,V5,What|T5]) ?
  rarebird([V2,V3,V4,V5,V6,What|T6]) ?
  rarebird([V2,V3,V4,V5,V6,V7,What|T7]) ?
    (user interrupt)
    [ Execution aborted ]
```

Prolog returns the names from the list, in order, as it should. Then, having been asked to find another, it goes on creating longer and longer lists of variables, looking for a list in the base that might match. Not surprisingly, this search is persistently unsuccessful and the generation of the lists soon fills up the available space in the computer. If the user had not interrupted the process, Prolog would have been forced to give up on its task (out of memory space) as it did in the example above.

Prolog's left-to-right processing means that the member requirement of the not__worthy rule is being processed before the list has been instantiated. To write more effective rules, have the list instantiation first (as it is in the note-worthy rule) and the membership processing second. This ordering makes intuitive sense in this problem so the programmer would probably have written the correct "noteworthy" form in the beginning. In general, however, first drafts of rules may not be in optimal order. A typical programmer, writing rules, will specify the requirements and then rearrange the form for improved effectiveness.

EXERCISES 5.4

1. Given this database

   ```
   author([k_wilhelm,juniper_time,fault_lines]).
   author([u_leguin,left_hand_of_darkness])
   author([l_m_alcott,little_women]).
   member(Element,[Element|_]).
   member(Element,[_|Tail]) :- member(Element,Tail).
   ```
   what will be Prolog's response to
   ```
   ?- author(List), member(juniper_time,List).
   ?- author(List), member(u_leguin,List).
   ?- author(List), member(little_women,List).
   ```
2. Given this database
   ```
   dwarves([sleepy,grumpy,happy,sneezy,dopey,bashful,doc]).
   no_beard([bashful,snow_white]).
   member(Element,[Element|_]).
   member(Element,[_|Tail]) :- member(Element,Tail).
   ```
   write a rule that will specify which dwarves have no beard.
3. Based on the description of the behavior of the not__worthy rule, you should be able to predict the responses to the query following this base, which has two rarebird lists in it. What will be the responses?
   ```
   rarebird([condor,crane,sparrow]).
   rarebird([cardinal,bluebird]).
   not_worthy(Bird) :- member(Bird,List), rarebird(List).
   member(Element,[Element|_]).
   member(Element,[_|Tail]) :- member(Element,Tail).
   ?- not_worthy(What).
   ```

5.5 PROCESSING LIST ELEMENTS

In addition to checking to see if an element is a member of a list, we might be interested in the element in a special location. The element in the front of the list is easy, as that is the head of the list.

```
front(Element,[Element|_]).
```

Finding the last element of a list requires working our way recursively to a single-element list.

```
last(Element,[Element]).
last(Element,[_|Tail]) :- last(Element,Tail).
```

Other, intermediate positions from the front can be specified by using a hybrid pattern, combining the "elements in a row" way of thinking with the "head/tail" way of handling lists of various sizes. Notice that the description of Prolog's processing of the not__worthy rule used this form. The first locations are specified and the remainder is allocated to the tail. For example,

```
third_place(Element,[_,_,Element|_]).
```

If we use the third place rule on a list that is not long enough to have a third place, Prolog will simply respond "no".

Another question we might ask is about successive elements. We can inquire about two elements being next to each other somewhere along the list.

```
next_to(First,Second,[First,Second|_]).
next_to(First,Second,[_|Tail]) :- next_to(First,Second,Tail).
```

The following is an example that shows the use of these rules for inquiring about particular elements in a program that includes the rarebird lists.

```
rarebird([condor,whooping_crane,dusky_seaside_sparrow]).
rarebird([blue_bird,cardinal]).

front(Element,[Element|_]).

last(Element,[Element]).
last(Element,[_|Tail]) :- last(Element,Tail).

third_place(Element,[_,_,Element|_]).

next_to(First,Second,[First,Second|_]).
next_to(First,Second,[_|Tail]) :- next_to(First,Second,Tail).
```

The query below is looking for the first bird in each rarebird list.

```
?- rarebird(List), front(Element,List).
Element = condor,
List = [condor,whooping_crane,dusky_seaside_sparrow];
Element = blue_bird,
List = [blue_bird,cardinal];
no
```

The next query is looking for the last bird in each list.

```
?- rarebird(List), last(Element,List).
Element = dusky_seaside_sparrow,
List = [condor,whooping_crane,dusky_seaside_sparrow];
Element = cardinal,
List = [blue_bird,cardinal];
no
```

This next query returns the third bird in the list. Since one list has only two birds, it has no third bird; the only response is from the longer list.

```
?- rarebird(List), third_place(Element,List).
Element = dusky_seaside_sparrow,
List = [condor,whooping_crane,dusky_seaside_sparrow];
no
```

This last query reports pairs of birds that are next to each other in the lists.

```
?- rarebird(List), next_to(One,Two,List).
One = condor,
List = [condor,whooping_crane,dusky_seaside_sparrow],
Two = whooping_crane ;

One = whooping_crane,
List = [condor,whooping_crane,dusky_seaside_sparrow],
Two = dusky_seaside_sparrow ;

One = blue_bird,
List = [blue_bird,cardinal],
Two = cardinal ;

no
```

EXERCISES 5.5

1. Given this database
   ```
   author([k_wilhelm,juniper_time,fault_lines]).
   author([u_leguin,left_hand_of_darkness]).
   author([l_m_alcott,little_women]).
   ```
   which rule from this section could you use to find out if any author has more than one book listed?
2. Write a rule using a rule from the rarebirds database that reports all author names (heads of list) in response to the query
   ```
   ?- author_names(Which).
   ```
3. In Exercises 5.1, you wrote two queries to test whether the last color in a predicate named rainbow was violet or purple. Rewrite those queries using rules from this section.

5.6 PROCESSING LISTS

Besides checking on the elements in lists, we often want to manipulate or build lists. To build a list, we can start with elements or we can start with lists to be combined into one larger list. Two tools for building lists from elements, **bagof** and **setof**, are discussed in Chapter 7, as they are built-in predicates. In this chapter, we will discuss a method for combining lists into a larger list, called appending. Append is not usually built into Prolog, so we will define it here.

Appending one list to another is a way of constructing a new list from two other lists. *Appending* means that the third, combined list is made up of the first list with the second list added on to its end. The way this is accomplished is recursively, with the recursive rule working down the first list, associating the successive head elements with elements in the equivalent position in the combined list.

```
append([Element|List1],List2,[Element|List3]) :-
        append(List1,List2,List3).
```

When the recursion reaches the end of the first list, the whole second list is added as the tail of the third list.

```
append([ ],List,List).
```

To visualize appending, consider again the stack of cards representing a list. To append two stacks of cards, first take cards from the first stack, one at a time from the top, and suspend them over the place the combined list will be stacked. When the whole of the first list is suspended, move the second list as a unit to the place where the combined list will be stacked. Then, unsuspend the elements above and let them settle into the combined, final list.

Figure 5.1

Appending Two Stacks of Cards

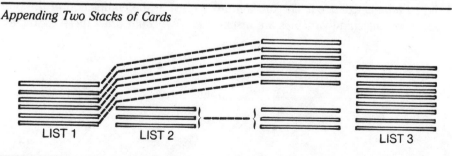

LIST 1   LIST 2   LIST 3

The first list being empty is the stopping case for the recursion. The rule combining the two cases is

```
append([ ],List,List).
append([Element|List1],List2,[Element|List3]) :-
    append(List1,List2,List3).

?- append([1,2,3],[a,b,c],Result).
Result = [1,2,3,a,b,c]

?- append([1,2,3],[3,4,5],Result).
Result = [1,2,3,3,4,5]

?- append(1,[a,b,c],Result).
no
```

This did not append because the first argument is an element, not a list.

```
?- append([ ],[a,b,c],Result).
Result = [a,b,c]
```

The empty list is a list so append works here.

Append can be used to find component lists as well as the combined list. Prolog can accept variables for any of the three lists that appear in the append predicate. This flexibility and power is available because the rules define the relationship without regard to which lists are known or unknown.

```
?- append([1,2,a],List,[1,2,a,b,c]).
List = [b,c]
?- append(List,[a,b,c],[1,2,a,b,c]).
List = [1,2]
```

Another analogy that may help you visualize these recursive definitions is that of a jointed telescope. Each time the append rule is used, imagine another sliding tube is extended. The tubes are collapsed at the completion of the process, when matching variables are instantiated. We could draw these examples.

```
?- append([1,2,a],List,[1,2,a,b,c]).
```

Figure 5.2

Telescope of Determining List2

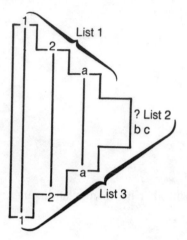

```
?- append(List,[a,b,c],[1,2,a,b,c]).
```

Figure 5.3

Telescope of Determining List1

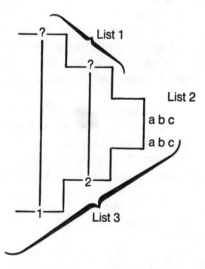

We can also use append to find all the possible sublists that would make up a combined list.

```
?- append(List1,List2,[a,b,c]).

List1 = [ ],
List2 = [a,b,c] ;

List1 = [a],
List2 = [b,c] ;

List1 = [a,b],
List2 = [c] ;

List1 = [a,b,c],
List2 = [ ] ;

no
```

We can use append in other list manipulation rules. For example, to reverse a list,

```
reverse([ ],[ ]).
reverse([Head|Tail],List) :- reverse(Tail,Result),
    append(Result,[Head],List).
```

Writing this rule presents the programmer with a decision. We have two rules of thumb about arranging the order of requirements components in a rule. One is that tail-recursion is preferred. The second is that predicates with fewer alternatives (like reverse) should be specified first. In this case, either arrangement works as long as we do not cause reverse to backtrack, looking for other answers. In backtracking, either can go out of control for some instantiations. Logically, however, there is only one reverse of a list, so backtracking with these rules should not arise. These two forms differ in their efficiency depending on which argument in reverse is known. Comparison of their efficiency is shown in the chapter supplement, Experimenting with Chapter 5.

This rule, combined with the append rules, will reverse either way. That is, the first argument can be known and the second found or the second known and the first found. Notice that append requires lists, so [Head] is the notation that must be used in that part of the rule. If we do not enclose Head in brackets, it will be an element, and append, which requires lists, will not work.

```
?- reverse([a,b,c],What).
What = [c,b,a]

?- reverse(List,[a,b]).
List = [b,a]
```

Add one more definition and this base will provide or check for palindromes. (This definition only handles palindromes with double center letters.)

```
palindrome(List1,List2) :- append(List1,List3,List2),
    reverse(List1,List3).

?- palindrome([a,b,c],Result).
Result = [a,b,c,c,b,a]

?- palindrome(Half,[a,b,c,c,b,a]).
Half = [a,b,c]
```

EXERCISES 5.6

1. Given this database
   ```
   rarebird([condor,crane,sparrow]).
   rarebird([bluebird,cardinal]).
   append([ ],List,List).
   append([Element|List1],List2,[Element|List3]) :-
       append(List1,List2,List3).
   reverse([ ],[ ]).
   reverse([Head|Tail],List) :- reverse(Tail,Result),
       append(Result,[Head],List).
   palindrome(List1,List2) :-
       append(List1,List3,List2),
       reverse(List1,List3).
   ```
   what will be the response to
   ```
   ?- rarebird(List), append([frigate_bird],List,Result).
   ?- rarebird(List), append(What,[cardinal],List).
   ?- rarebird(List), append(List,List,Result).
   ?- rarebird(L1), rarebird(L2), append(L1,L2,Result).
   ```
2. Given the database above, what will be the response to
   ```
   ?- rarebird(List), reverse(List,Result).
   ?- rarebird(List), palindrome(List,Result).
   ?- rarebird(List), palindrome(Half,List).
   ```
3. Write a rule that will create a palindrome without duplicating the last element in the source list. For example,
   ```
   odd_pal([a,b,c],Result).
   Result = [a,b,c,b,a]
   ```

5.7 GENERALIZING ON LISTS

All the lists we have looked at so far have been made up of specific objects. That is, all the elements have been constant names. Lists can be used more generally than that: elements can be variables, allowing more flexible use through instantiation; elements can themselves be lists, allowing an overall hierarchical organization of elements.

The following example shows how lists of lists can be used to specify components of a larger problem. The database in this example uses combinations of lists to specify courses a computer science student should take for a specific semester. It is organized so that a student could find out general recommendations for courses to take or confirm that planned courses meet the recommendations.

The recommended list is made up of a core list and an option list for each semester. The core list is a combination of computer science and math courses, while the option list includes language courses and liberal arts courses. The facts at the end of the base specify individual courses in some cases and, in others, lists of courses that meet the requirements. By using lists, options can be presented as a group in response to a query. If each course were in a separate fact, backtracking would be necessary to display all choices.

```
append([ ],List,List).
append([Element|List1],List2,[Element|List3]) :-
     append(List1,List2,List3).
recommend(Semester,Classes) :-   required(Semester,Corelist),
                                 option(Semester,Liberallist),
                                 append(Corelist,Liberallist,
                                        Classes).
required(Semester,Corelist) :-   cs(Semester,Listcs),
                                 math(Semester,Listmt),
                                 append(Listcs,Listmt,
                                        Corelist).
option(Semester,Liberallist) :-  lang(Semester,Listlg),
                                 lb_art(Semester,Listla),
                                 append(Listlg,Listla,
                                        Liberallist).
cs(one,[cs304]).
cs(two,[cs315]).
cs(three,[[cs410,cs328]]).
math(one,[math808a]).
math(two,[math808b]).
math(three,[one_of_math,[311,340,427,343,362]]).
lang(one,[eng_306,lang_506]).
lang(two,[lang_507]).
lang(three,[eng_316]).
lb_art(one,[ ]).
lb_art(two,[elective_from,social_science]).
lb_art(three,[elective_from,[history,government]]).

?- recommend(one,Classes).
Classes = [cs304,math808a,eng_306,lang_506]
yes

?- recommend(two,Classes).
Classes = [cs315,math808b,lang_507,elective_from,
   social_science]
yes

?- recommend(three,Classes).
Classes = [[cs410,cs328],one_of_math,[311,340,427,343,362],
   eng_316,elective_from,[history,government]]
yes
```

In working with lists that may contain lists along with simple objects as elements, we sometimes need a way of determining whether an element is a list or not. The rule that identifies a list comes directly from the list definition: the empty list is a list; an object is a list if it has a head and a tail.

```
is_a_list([ ]).
is_a_list([_|_]).
```

1. Given these lists, specify the head and tail of each list.
```
[one,[two]]
[[one],[two]]
[[one],two]
[one,[two,three]]
[one,two,[three]]
[one,two,three]
```
2. What will be the instantiation reported for
```
reverse([H|T],[one,two]).
reverse([H|T],[[one],[two]]).
```

SUMMARY
Prolog lists provide a mechanism for grouping objects. Lists are made up of elements; in Prolog we need to be able to manipulate both the lists as wholes and the individual elements in the lists. Individual elements can be accessed either through their position in the list or by using the head/tail separation of the list which allows access to the first element of a specified list. A list either has a head and tail or else it is the special, empty list.

Recursion provides the basis for list processing tools, such as membership in a list, appending of lists and analysis of lists for particular elements.

SYNTAX SUMMARY
```
empty list [ ]
list [Element1,Element2,..ElementN]
head/tail  [Head|Tail]
```
    head is an element
    tail is a list

hybrid form (enumerating some elements and a tail)
```
[Element1, Element2,...|Tail]
```

EXPERIMENTING WITH CHAPTER 5

Purpose:
To see different instantiation patterns in rearranged predicates
comparisons of efficiency for different patterns

Processing patterns and relative efficiency of different predicate arrangements
can be seen by using trace during queries. Below is a Prolog.log showing the
two forms of the reverse rule we discussed earlier in the chapter. We can
count the number of matches needed to process the query in each case as a
way of comparing these forms. The palindrome rules also are the basis for
some interesting experiments. Responses differ depending on the arrangement
of palindrome's requirements and on the definition of reverse that is with it in
the database.

```
Prolog-10   version 3.3
Copyright (C) 1981 by D. Warren, F. Pereira and L. Byrd

| ?- ['revers.1st'].

revers.1st consulted   90 words   0.09 sec.

yes
| ?- listing.

append([],_1,_1).
append([_1|_2],_3,[_1|_4]) :-
   append(_2,_3,_4).

reverse([],[]).
reverse([_1|_2],_3) ·-
   reverse(_2,_4),
   append(_4,[_1],_3).

yes
| ?- trace.
Debug mode switched on.

yes
| ?- reverse([a,b],L).
   (1) 0 Call : reverse([a,b],_38) ?
   (2) 1 Call : reverse([b],_103) ?
   (3) 2 Call : reverse([],_115) ?
   (3) 2 Exit : reverse([],[])
   (4) 2 Call : append([],[b],_103) ?
   (4) 2 Exit : append([],[b],[b])
   (2) 1 Exit : reverse([b],[b])
   (5) 1 Call : append([b],[a],_38) ?
   (6) 2 Call : append([],[a],_143) ?
   (6) 2 Exit : append([],[a],[a])
   (5) 1 Exit : append([b],[a],[b,a])
   (1) 0 Exit : reverse([a,b],[b,a])
```

```
L = [b,a]

yes
| ?- trace.

yes
| ?- reverse(L,[a,b]).
  (1) 0 Call : reverse(_24,[a,b]) ?
  (2) 1 Call : reverse(_101,_103) ?
  (2) 1 Exit : reverse([],[])
  (3) 1 Call : append([],[_100],[a,b]) ?
  (3) 1 Fail : append([],[_100],[a,b])
  (2) 1 Redo : reverse([],[]) ?
  (4) 2 Call : reverse(_113,_115) ?
  (4) 2 Exit : reverse([],[])
  (5) 2 Call : append([],[_112],_103) ?
  (5) 2 Exit : append([],[_112],[_112])
  (2) 1 Exit : reverse([_112],[_112])
  (6) 1 Call : append([_112],[_100],[a,b]) ?
  (7) 2 Call : append([],[_100],[b]) ?
  (7) 2 Exit : append([],[b],[b])
  (6) 1 Exit : append([a],[b],[a,b])
  (1) 0 Exit : reverse([b,a],[a,b])

L = [b,a]

yes
| ?- [-'append.1st'].

append.1st reconsulted   4 words   0.08 sec.

yes
| ?- listing.

append([],_1,_1).
append([_1|_2],_3,[_1|_4]) :-
  append(_2,_3,_4).

reverse([],[]).
reverse([_1|_2],_3) :-
  append(_4,[_1],_3),
  reverse(_2,_4).

yes
| ?- trace.
Debug mode switched on.
```

```
yes
| ?- reverse([a,b],L).
  (1) 0 Call : reverse([a,b],_38) ?
  (2) 1 Call : append(_103,[a],_38) ?
  (2) 1 Exit : append([],[a],[a])
  (3) 1 Call : reverse([b],[]) ?
  (4) 2 Call : append(_124,[b],[]) ?
  (4) 2 Fail : append(_124,[b],[])
  (3) 1 Fail : reverse([b],[])
  (2) 1 Redo : append([],[a],[a]) ?
  (5) 2 Call : append(_113,[a],_115) ?
  (5) 2 Exit : append([],[a],[a])
  (2) 1 Exit : append([_112],[a],[_112,a])
  (6) 1 Call : reverse([b],[_112]) ?
  (7) 2 Call : append(_136,[b],[_112]) ?
  (7) 2 Exit : append([],[b],[b])
  (8) 2 Call : reverse([],[]) ?
  (8) 2 Exit : reverse([],[])
  (6) 1 Exit : reverse([b],[b])
  (1) 0 Exit : reverse([a,b],[b,a])

L = [b,a]

yes
| ?- trace.

yes
| ?- reverse(L,[a,b]).
  (1) 0 Call : reverse(_24,[a,b]) ?
  (2) 1 Call : append(_103,[_100],[a,b]) ?
  (3) 2 Call : append(_113,[_100],[b]) ?
  (3) 2 Exit : append([],[b],[b])
  (2) 1 Exit : append([a],[b],[a,b])
  (4) 1 Call : reverse(_101,[a]) ?
  (5) 2 Call : append(_136,[_133],[a]) ?
  (5) 2 Exit : append([],[a],[a])
  (6) 2 Call : reverse(_134,[]) ?
  (6) 2 Exit : reverse([],[])
  (4) 1 Exit : reverse([a],[a])
  (1) 0 Exit : reverse([b,a],[a,b])

L = [b,a]

yes
```

EXERCISES CHAPTER 5 ▐████████████████████████████

1. Identify the Prolog concept or concepts described by each phrase below.
   a) An ordered sequence of constants, variables or lists.
   b) The repetition process that is the basis for many predicates that process lists.
   c) Why using the head/tail notation for lists is more flexible.
   d) In a rule like append, which of the arguments may be the unspecified argument when the process is begun.
   e) Two ways lists may be accessed.
   f) A way individual elements in a list can be specified.
2. Using the Prolog database given below, find all possible answers for the queries below.
   ```
   pen([cat,[dog,hen]]).
   pen([[cat,dog,chicken],hen,pig]).
   pen([cat,dog,hen,pig,[chicken|[ox,bull]]]).
   ?- pen([X|Y]).
   ?- pen(_,_,_,_,[X|Y]).
   ?- pen([_|X]).
   ?- pen([_,_|X]).
   ```
3. Each of the next 5 questions gives a Prolog sentence followed by several statements. For each question find ALL of the statements that are true about the Prolog sentence.
   a) `carpet(hall,beige).`
      1) This is a rule.
      2) This is a fact.
      3) This could be the stopping condition for recursion.
      4) This uses list notation.
   b) `need_ice :- weather(warm), picnic(Day).`
      1) This is a rule.
      2) This is a fact.
      3) This could be the stopping condition for recursion.
      4) This uses list notation.
   c) `classes([german,physics,calculus,composition]).`
      1) This is a rule.
      2) This is a fact.
      3) This could be the stopping condition for recursion
      4) This uses list notation.
   d) `owned(Property,Person) :-`
      `            bought(Property,Person,builder).`
      1) This is a rule.
      2) This is a fact.
      3) This could be the stopping condition for recursion.
      4) This uses list notation.

   e) `classes([H|Tail]).`

      1) This list could contain 2 elements.

      2) This list could contain more than 2 elements.

      3) This list could contain 0 elements.

      4) This list could contain 1 element.

4. Write Prolog programs for these problems.

   a) Write a database that includes several lists as arguments to the predicate "trip". Each list should specify the streets you travel on a specific trip around your town.

   b) Write rules and queries that will find out if you use the same street as part of two trips.

   c) Write a new database for palindrome that makes palindromes with an uneven number of elements, but instead of modifying palindrome, modify reverse so that the reversed component is one shorter than the original.

   d) Write a database that has a rule which accepts a list and two elements as arguments. The rule should go through the list and replace every occurrence of the first element with the second element. That is:

```
?- swap(a,z,[a,b,a,c],New_list).
New_list = [z,b,z,c]
```

PART II

Advanced Topics

How Prolog Is Like and Unlike Other Languages

PROGRAMMING CONCEPTS

Being fluent in one programming language usually helps a person in learning another language. However, many people who have experience in computer programming find that this prior experience interferes to some degree with their learning of Prolog. While many of the concepts these programmers already know, such as system organization and file handling, are helpful, other concepts are not. Two facets of the programmer's prior knowledge create problems:

1. their model of what a program is
2. the components they expect to find making up the language.

THE PROGRAM MODEL

Procedural Model

The model that these programmers have learned (and been taught) is "the program as recipe." In this model, the program is an algorithm that specifies carefully and explicitly the steps the computer must take to create a result. Results, be they intermediate or final, are recorded in the computer memory in labelled locations, which are called variables. The programmer's responsibility consists of specifying the correct sequence of steps and being sure that correct values are stored under correct variable names. This model, which is called the von Neumann model, is useful for programming in procedural languages, such as Pascal, BASIC, and C.

Declarative Model

Programming requirements are different, however, for a declarative language like Prolog. The primary responsibility of the Prolog programmer is to give a correct definition of the problem and its components. The definition is made up of facts and rules. Each fact or rule is a logical sentence that makes an assertion about the problem. Output is generated when a query is made of the facts and rules. The output is derived from the definition. The Prolog system, not the explicit instruction of the Prolog programmer, controls the processing that produces the output.

Program Processing

Say, for example, one were designing a program module to search a group of records to find the last name of a person whose first name is Mary and who lives in Austin. In Prolog, such a program might contain a set of facts of the following form.

```
person (mary,bain,dallas).
person(mary,jones,austin).
person(john,jones,austin).
person(mary,smith,austin).
```

The facts are a part of the program rather than a separate component called "data". That is, the program is the database and vice versa. The facts would be used along with an interactive question of the form:

```
?- person(mary,Last_name,austin).
```

This would precipitate a response

```
Last_name = jones
```

The response returns a constant value (marked by beginning with a lower-case letter) that when used in place of the variable (upper-case letter) in the question, yields a statement true according to the base. The list of facts and the question are the totality of this Prolog program. Rules, which appear in the database along with the facts, are the other component of Prolog programs. Rules contain a head and a body, separated by the composite symbol, colon-dash. The head of the rule expresses a conclusion and the body of the rule specifies the condition or conditions required for the conclusion. Rules typically include variables. For example,

```
schedule(skiing,Month) :- winter(Month)
```

This rule could be read "Schedule skiing during a month if that month is in the winter".

Pattern Matching

A program comparable to the example above might be written in Pascal using records. Assuming the records are stored in an array, the search module might look like this:

```
Procedure Find(Base:DataArray; Var Sought:LastNameType);
Var Index:Integer;
Begin
  Index := 1;
  While NOT(Base[Index].FirstName=Mary
        AND Base[Index].Local=Austin)
    Index := Index + 1;
  Sought := Base[Index].LastName
End;
```

The specific directions that the Pascal programmer gives in the program instruct the system to look through the records one by one until the matching record is found. When using Prolog, this kind of search for a matching pattern is implicit, and is, in fact, the basis for all Prolog programs. Components of a Prolog program are general record structures. Under Prolog's control, the search for matching patterns proceeds through the records from the top to the bottom of the database. The Prolog programmer exerts some control over the processing by choosing the order of the components in the database. If, in the above Prolog example, the fourth line had come first, the result returned would have been different.

```
Last_name = smith
```

There are some special extensions to the logical core of Prolog that programmers can use to add a more procedural flavor to a program. Fundamentally, however, a Prolog program does not express the procedural "Do this" but rather says "This is what's known; this is what the answer should look like; find it".

LANGUAGE COMPONENTS

Variables and Values

In the Pascal example above, several of the instructions are assignment statements. The Pascal programmer specifies when values will be stored in variables. The assignment statement is a fundamental part of procedural languages and one that experienced programmers expect to find in a programming language.

The pattern-matching process in Prolog also involves the association of specific constant values with individual variable names (called instantiation), but again it is Prolog rather than the programmer who directs it. Thus, there is no assignment statement in Prolog. Values and variables are associated by their matching in patterns. There are some supplements to the core Prolog language that allow programmers to effect assignments, but again these are beyond the descriptive core of Prolog. Rather than simple assignments, they are ways of building Prolog structures.

Control Statements

The second component that programmers expect to find in a language are control statements. In the Pascal program above, the While..Do loop controls iteration. Instructions for looping, conditionals and transfer to subroutines appear in procedural languages. The transfer of control that these instructions accomplish in procedural programming is built into the Prolog system. Thus, conditionals and loops do not appear in Prolog programs as they do in procedural languages. Alternate choices are accomplished through failure and backtracking. Repeated application is accomplished through backtracking and recursion.

Alternation

For example, one might have two rules defining a comfortable place to live.

```
comfortable(Place) :- climate(Place,hot),
                      house(Place,airconditioned).
comfortable(Place) :- climate(Place,moderate).
```

The rules can be read

1. A place is comfortable if the climate there is hot and the house there is air-conditioned.
2. A place is comfortable if the climate there is moderate.

Both these rules would be in the database at the same time. Multiple rules defining the same outcome provide alternatives. In this case, rule 1 or rule 2 can be used to determine that a place is comfortable.

During Prolog's pattern-matching process, the rules are checked in the order they are listed. If the conditions in the first rule are not true, the system backtracks to try the next rule. This mechanism allows complex conditionals to be expressed, with the multiple rule form providing an easy-to-understand specification.

If no rule succeeds, the Prolog system reports the failure. Failure of rules allows for negation in a Prolog program. It is only negation within the facts and rules provided in the program. Prolog assumes that the given program contains all true assertions; this is called the closed-world assumption.

Repetition

Recursion is frequently used in Prolog. Its structure can be built with multiple rules, including one or more stopping cases and one or more recursive cases. For example:

```
ancestor(Older,Younger) :- parent(Older,Younger).
ancestor(Older,Younger) :- parent(Older,Middle),
                           ancestor(Middle,Younger).
```

These two rules can be tested and used repeatedly for matching because the scope of a variable is limited to the sentence in which it appears. Many Prolog implementations recognize tail-recursion and optimize it into iteration. Thus, where appropriate, efficiency can be improved without requiring the programmer to build the iterative structure.

Rules, single or multiple, can be used both to check (confirm the truth of) a fact or to generate values that are confirmed in the facts. Thus, the multiple rule shown above (along with related facts in the database) above could be used to confirm

```
?- ancestor(adam,bob).
```

to find an ancestor

```
?- ancestor(Who,bob).
```

to find a descendant

```
?- ancestor(adam,Who).
```

or to generate through backtracking all ancestor-descendant pairs

```
?- ancestor(Senior,Junior).
```

Note that, unlike procedure parameters in many languages, the variables are not limited to being either input or output parameters. Any parameter can take the role of input or output. Rule definitions may be processed more efficiently for some input/output patterns than others.

LISTS

Prolog has special pattern notation for list structures, which, combined with backtracking and recursion creates convenient list manipulation. The notation is

```
[Variable1|Variable2].
```

where Variable1 is the first element in the list (the head), Variable2 is a list of the remaining elements (the tail), and the square-bracketed structure is the whole list. Thus the list constructor and the list selector are implicit within the pattern. For example,

```
append([],List,List).
append([Element|List1],List2,[Element|List3]) :-
        append(List1,List2,List3).
```

This append rule can be used to combine two lists into one, to break one list into all its component-list-pairs, or to return or confirm a sublist. In processing a complex set of specifications, Prolog attempts its matches left to right through the rule. Procedural programmers, accustomed to concerning themselves about sequence of processing, tend to assume that one component must be "completed" before processing can move on. Prolog does not require instantiation of all variables in one component before proceeding to the next. Rather, Prolog returns the most general match that meets the current specificatons.

CALCULATIONS

Prolog can be used to do arithmetic. For example, the factorial function can be represented recursively.

```
factorial(0,1).
factorial(N,Value) :- PreN is N-1,
                      factorial(PreN,Subvalue),
                      Value is Subvalue*N.
```

Most Prolog implementations do only integer arithmetic although in some cases, real arithmetic is available. Prolog is not convenient for "number crunching". Additionally, the special operator **is**, which allows a form of assignment, requires there be no uninstantiated variable in the expression to its right, so rules using it are limited in the roles of input and output parameters. The rule above will work for

```
?- factorial(3,Value).
```

but not for

```
?- factorial(N,6).
```

Using arithmetic to derive information from a database is a more appropriate Prolog task than is generating numeric values. For example, given a database with facts about individuals birth dates, one could write a rule like

```
can_vote(Person) :- birthyear(Person,Year),
                    Age is (1986 - Year),
                    Age >= 18.
```

VIEW OF PROGRAMMING

Logic and Control

Most experienced programmers, learning Prolog and therefore having to alter their view of what progamming means, typically choose one of two images. The first is to view Prolog as a "higher-level" language, a language in which specifications are turned into the actual "program" by the Prolog system. The second view recognizes that, while some programs are algorithms, not all need be. Prolog programs are theorems, specifying known rules and facts. When a query is made in the program, an additional clause is combined with the theorem and a proof is generated. The proof is what produces the answer to the query.

In either of these views, control in the program is separated from the logical component. In a program, the knowledge of relationships and outcomes is its logical component. The directions expressing the process for using this knowledge to find a problem solution make up the control component. The Prolog programmer's central concern is to express the logical component. When this has been done, modifications can be made for improving process performance without invalidating the logic component. This separation of logic and control has two advantages:

1. The cognitive load on the programer is reduced, so that original programs can be written with less time and effort
2. The logic component, being free of control information, is easy to read and understand, providing the attendant advantages of improved correctness, maintainability and reuse.

Program Development

Prolog allows development of program units for subproblems of a task. Design and testing of modules is facilitated by Prolog's interactive programming environment and interpreted translation. Prolog, however, does not have any mechanism for information hiding or encapsulation. All the names in a Prolog program are global and the complete database is accessible at all times. Searches for a specific clause always begin at the top of the base and there is no "most recent referent" structure as there is in some procedural languages.

Because names are global, the programmer must avoid using the same name and arity for predicates with different meanings. This is usually not a problem in small programs, but in large programs or programs written jointly by several people, it often is.

For further reading on these topics, see Backus [1978], Kowalski [1974b] and Warren, Pereira and Pereira [1977], listed in Appendix B.

Improving the Efficiency of Prolog Programs

The purpose of this chapter is to help the learner:
- understand the different views of
  descriptive or declarative semantics.
  prescriptive or procedural semantics.
- recognize the control mechanisms in Prolog.
- consider alternatives that improve efficiency of Prolog programs.
- understand and be able to use the cut in modifying control.

6.1 DESCRIPTIVE VERSUS PRESCRIPTIVE

In the beginning of this book, we discussed a Prolog program as a base of facts and rules that describe a world. The facts and rules specified things that are true in that particular world. Queries made of the database asked Prolog to derive conclusions about the world, or to provide us with object names that made a particular statement true. When we take this view of a Prolog program, we are looking at the *declarative* or *descriptive* semantics (meaning) of the program.

In Chapter 4, we focused on the process Prolog uses to analyze the questions and the database. In answering our questions, we saw that Prolog follows a sequence of steps, matching predicates and arguments, instantiating variables and backtracking when necessary. If we extend our thinking along this line, we can view a Prolog program as a series of directions to Prolog, telling it how to go about discovering the answer to our query. The way we write our rules and questions affects the process Prolog will follow. The programmer becomes a direction-giver rather than a world-definer. When we look at a Prolog program as a set of instructions to be carried out, we are considering the *procedural* or *prescriptive* semantics of the program.

In looking at the prescriptive semantics of a program, we are recognizing that the program will be processed by Prolog on a machine. As part of the processing, Prolog uses methods that the programmer knows about and takes advantage of. For example, matching is done starting at the top of the database, predicates in rules are attacked left-to-right, and backtracking takes up where it left off, uninstantiating variables. The programmer builds on these Prolog methods to write a program that will behave effectively.

The facet of a program that concerns how a program will work is called *processing control* or simply *control*. As we have seen, control in a Prolog program depends on both the Prolog system (with its underlying machine) and the order of the program components which the programmer specifies.

In considering efficiency for a Prolog program, we must recognize that we are looking at the prescriptive, not the descriptive semantics of the program. Meanwhile, the descriptive view of the program should not be forgotten, as it is of fundamental importance in logic programming. One of the advantages, however, of Prolog programming is that we can consider the logic and the control in a program as separate matters. The descriptive semantics of a program refers to the analysis of the problem to be solved. The prescriptive semantics refers to the processes by which the problem is to be solved. Conceptually, the Prolog programmer is concerned with the descriptive semantics; practically, he or she must also be concerned with prescriptive semantics.

As an example of descriptive versus prescriptive semantics, consider the multiple rule for appending lists that we saw in Chapter 5. First, recall the idea: append means that the combined list will be made of the first list with the second list added on at the first list's end. We recognize that in the special case where the first list is empty, the combined list will be just the same as the second list. We also see that in the general case, the element that is the head of the first list will be the head of the combined list and that the tail of the first list with the second list appended to it will be the tail of the combined list. We wrote the Prolog rules for this definition.

```
append([ ],List,List).
append([Element|List1],List2,[Element|List3]) :-
        append(List1,List2,List3).
```

Descriptively, we can see that this rule gives us a definition of what append means. The two rules describe the two cases: when the first list is empty; when the first list is not empty (and therefore has a head and tail). Between the two parts, the relationship append is totally defined.

In contrast, looking at append prescriptively, we must consider a sequential process that consists of copying constant values from one list to another. Consider the case where list1 and list2 are given and the combined list is being created. The elements from the first list are copied into the combined list, one at a time in order. When all of list1 has been copied, list2 is copied as a whole on the end of the partially built combined list.

Consider the second case where list1 and the combined list are known and list2 is being found. Elements in list1 and the combined list are matched from the beginning of the lists until all of list1 has been matched. Then the rest of the combined list is copied as list2.

In the third case, where list2 and the combined list are known, list1 will be created. Elements from the combined list are skipped over until the remainder of the combined list matches list2, then the elements that have been skipped over are copied into list1.

Notice that to consider the append process prescriptively, one must think about the different cases separately. The descriptive view covers all three cases because the rules express the definition of the relationship.

Goals

Like the append example, any Prolog rule can be read two ways: as a description of relationships between objects or as a prescription for carrying out some task.

When we ask a question of Prolog, we are setting up a *goal* for Prolog to try to satisfy. The goal Prolog is processing has been *activated*. Descriptively, this goal asks Prolog to confirm that the relationship in the query is true in the world description that the database represents, or in the case of a query with variables, report variable instantiations that satisfy the goal. Thus, if Prolog is able to find facts and rules that allow the conclusion in the goal, we can say the goal is *satisfied* or that it has *succeeded*. If a particular goal cannot be satisfied, that goal has *failed*.

While trying to satisfy a goal, Prolog is often required to establish intermediate goals. These goals are activated in turn as processing continues. When the goal that Prolog is trying to satisfy is the head of a rule, the requirements in the body of the rule must be met. Thus these one or more components become intermediate goals or *subgoals* of the head goal.

When a particular goal has been satisfied, it has been matched or *unified* with a fact, or with the head of a rule in which the subgoals have been satisfied. The unification may later be rejected when failure of another goal causes backtracking. For example:

```
shade(sox,green).
shade(sox,black).
color(shoes,black).
color(shoes,white).
mono_feet(Hue) :- shade(sox,Hue),
    color(Footgear,Hue).
?- mono_feet(Tone).
```

First, mono_feet is matched to the head of the rule. Since Tone and Hue both are variables, no instantiations to constants are done. Rather

```
shade(sox,Hue).
```

is taken as a subgoal and a search for its match is started. It matches with

```
shade(sox,green).
```

This subgoal is now satisfied and Hue is instantiated to green. Prolog's processing moves to the right in the rule and a new subgoal is set up:

```
color(Footgear,green).
```

The search through the database does not find a match for a color predicate with green as the second object, so the goal fails.

The failure of the second subgoal forces Prolog to backtrack, giving up the match and instantiations from the success of the first subgoal. Prolog searches on from the place of the rejected unification, trying to *re-satisfy* the first subgoal in the rule.

In this case, the next unification of

    `shade(sox,Hue).`

will instantiate Hue to black, and the goal

    `color(Footgear,black).`

will succeed with Footgear instantiated to shoes.

Since both the subgoals in the rule have succeeded, the original goal

    `mono_feet(Tone).`

has also succeeded, and the instantiation

    `Tone = black`

will be reported. If we respond to this report with a semicolon, backtracking begins again. Another match is sought for

    `color(Footgear,black).`

but resatisfying this goal fails. Backtracking releases the instantiation of Hue to black and Prolog tries to re-satisfy the earlier goal

    `shade(sox,Hue).`

This also cannot be satisfied, so there are no more ways the goal

    `mono_feet(Tone).`

can succeed with the rule we have been using. A further search finds no more ways for mono_feet to possibly succeed, so Prolog reports its failure, with a "no."

In introducing the idea of Prolog goals which succeed or fail, we are revisiting the concepts that were discussed in Chapter 4. There we talked about the methods that Prolog uses to respond to our queries. Here again we are talking about the methods Prolog uses. The difference between these two discussions lies in our perspective on the Prolog program.

In Chapter 4, our view of a program was strictly as a definition. The facts and rules we provided described a complete world and specified what was true in that world. Our view of Prolog's processing there was that Prolog, in responding to our query, had to follow certain methods to discover correct responses to give us.

When we speak of goals in Prolog, we are taking a more dynamic view of a Prolog program. We view the process Prolog uses to get from our query to its responses as a path to be traveled, with goals and subgoals as milestones along the path. Each goal must be activated and Prolog succeeds or fails in attaining the goals along the path. For example, to return to the database above

```
shade(sox,green).
shade(sox,black).
color(shoes,black).
color(shoes,white).
mono_feet(Hue) :- shade(sox,Hue),
    color(Footgear,Hue).
```

We could diagram the goals and subgoals from the earlier example of ?- mono__feet(Hue) as in Figure 6.1.

Figure 6.1

Goals and Subgoals in mono__feet(Hue)

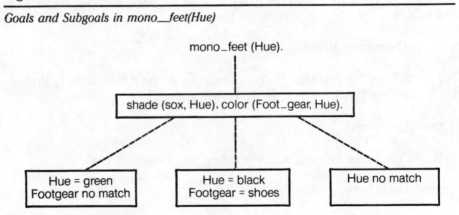

Using a diagram such as this, we can trace attempts at meeting goals by moving down in the diagram and trace backtracking by moving up. A similar diagram, with the addition of arrows, shows the path that Prolog follows in processing the goals. In this format, the whole process of the earlier example would look like Figure 6.2.

Figure 6.2

Processing Pattern for mono__feet(Hue).

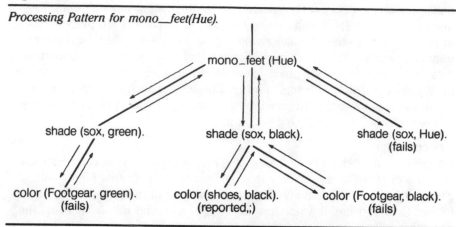

1. Write two brief paragraphs, one which explains this program descriptively, and one which explains it procedurally.

```
reverse([ ],[ ]).
reverse([Head|Tail],List) :- reverse(Tail,Result),
        append(Result,[Head],List).
append([ ],List,List).
append([Element|List1],List2,[Element|List3]) :-
        append(List1,List2,List3).
```

2. Draw a diagram of the processing pattern for this base and query.

```
loud(sirens).
loud(music).
can_buy(house).
can_buy(music).
?- can_buy(What),loud(What).
```

6.2 PARALLELISM

The diagram at the end of the last section points out another characteristic of a Prolog program. We have been assuming that a computer under Prolog's control will be doing only one thing at a time; it will be following a single path attempting to succeed at a sequence of goals. In our diagram, this path starts at the top and goes down branches starting with the ones shown to the left in the diagram. The place where facts appear in the diagram is determined by where they appear in the database.

In looking for any (or all) possible instantiations for Hue, however, there is no reason for investigation of the middle path in the diagram to wait until the first path is done. These paths could be traveled in parallel. To process Prolog in parallel requires that the underlying Prolog/computer system be different from that we have been discussing. Parallel Prolog systems are an important area in research and development. Several of the articles and books listed in Appendix B discuss this topic further. Considering such systems is beyond the scope of this book, but every Prolog programmer should be aware of the inherent parallelism in a Prolog program.

Procedures

An even more process-oriented view of a Prolog program is to consider each rule in a program as a *procedure* that outlines the activity that Prolog will carry out in finding an answer. The answer will be in the form of a value (object) for a variable. If a rule has the head of a second rule in its body, the procedure calls on the second rule as a subprocedure.

When a procedure calls a second procedure, it can give the second procedure some already instantiated variables and can get back from the second procedure instantiations for more variables. With Prolog procedures, any of the variables can have values sent along when a procedure is called or returned from the called procedure. In the vocabulary of procedures, these values are called *parameters*. They can be specific values or uninstantiated variables.

This view of a Prolog program is extremely prescriptive. It sees a program as a recipe or algorithm that specifies the behavior of the computer under control of a program. This view of a program disregards the descriptive component of the program.

Logic Plus Control

A Prolog program that is going to be carried out on a computer has both descriptive and prescriptive semantics. The descriptive semantics is made of the facts and rules, and the meaning to the programmer of the description of the problem. The prescriptive semantics is built from the programmer's awareness of how the Prolog/computer system will process the program it is given and from the choices the programmer makes in the expression and ordering of facts and rules.

A Prolog program is written descriptively so that the logic can be checked and correctness assured. The meaning of the program can be understood without regard to how the Prolog/computer system will properly carry out the program. Then the same program can be considered prescriptively to be sure the realities of the system will properly carry out the program. Here, too, efficiency in time and space for computing can be considered. The Prolog program can be modified to improve its behavior as long as the logical correctness remains. That is, the prescriptive semantics changes while the descriptive semantics remains unchanged.

Earlier, in Chapter 4, we discussed a few rules of thumb for avoiding some problems with recursion and for improving efficiency. One of those rules suggested putting the recursive component as far right in a definition as possible. That is

```
<predicate> :- <some constraint>,
               <predicate with different variables>.
```

Descriptively, this definition has the same meaning in whichever order the requirements components appear. The definition can be written either way and analyzed to be sure it is a correct definition. If the definition is going to be used on a computer, pragmatic concerns arise and the definition must be viewed prescriptively. At this time, the programmer must choose a specific order for the components.

Another suggestion for limiting the work Prolog must do was to arrange components in the body of a rule so that the predicate that appears first is the one with the fewest possible matches. That is, if the goal is to have matching shoes and sox out of three pair of shoes and twenty pair of sox, it is usually better to choose a pair of shoes and then search for matching sox than to start with the sox. That is, you would ask the question

```
?- color(shoes,Hue), shade(sox,Hue).
```

if you have fewer predicates that specify the color of shoes and use

```
?- shade(sox,Hue), color(shoes,Hue).
```

if you have fewer predicates about the shade of sox. Again, the definition of matching shoes and sox does not depend on the order, but it may be important practically for Prolog. It means that fewer false starts at matching the complete rule will be processed.

Another place where rule structure affects Prolog efficiency is in the direction of use of a definition. Descriptively, a Prolog definition can specify results in any argument location. For example,

```
ancestor(Oldperson,Youngperson) :- ...... ...
```

can be used to find Oldperson if Youngperson is given

```
?- ancestor(Who,jean).
```

or to find Youngperson when Oldperson is given

```
?- ancestor(george,Who).
```

Depending on how the definition of ancestor is written, one of these requests is apt to require a lot more work of the computer than the other. If the Prolog programmer knows the predicate will be used primarily one way, then the definition can be put in order to cater to that use.

For similar reasons, other definitions of predicates may be written to narrow the use of predicates to only the tasks they do efficiently. Another predicate, descendant, could be defined that works more efficiently when the Oldperson is specified and the Youngperson sought. In building related definitions like these, however, one should carefully avoid building an unwanted oscillating recursion.

EXERCISES 6.2

1. Write two definitions of ancestor that are descriptively valid, choose one as prescriptively preferable and explain why.
2. Write a database of four facts, a rule for ancestor and a rule for descendant.

6.3 CUT
Prolog has a special goal called the **cut** that can be used to modify the prescriptive semantics of a Prolog program. The *cut*, which is written !, is a special goal; when activated, it succeeds immediately but only once. If backtracking causes processing to return to the cut, the cut will not only fail but will cause the failure of its parent goal. The *parent goal* is the goal that called the rule in which the cut appeared. For example:

```
holiday(tuesday,july_4).
weather(tuesday,fair).
weekend(saturday).
weekend(sunday).
make(potato_salad,Day) :- picnic(Day).
picnic(Day) :- weather(Day,fair), !, weekend(Day)
picnic(Day) :- holiday(Day,july_4).

?- make(potato_salad,tuesday).
no
```

In processing this query, Prolog sets up the goal of finding a match for the predicate in the question. It finds the match in the rule where it instantiates Day to tuesday. This next goal activated requires Prolog to find a match for

```
picnic(tuesday).
```

Prolog makes the match to the first rule that has picnic(Day) as its head. Its subgoal

```
weather(tuesday,fair).
```

is activated and succeeds. Moving right,

```
!
```

is activated and succeeds immediately. Next

```
weekend(tuesday).
```

is activated. This goal fails, so backtracking is begun. The backtracking moves to the goal

```
!
```

which having succeeded once, now fails. At the same time it also fails the parent goal, which is

```
picnic(tuesday).
```

Since this goal fails,

```
make(potato_salad,tuesday).
```

also fails and Prolog reports "no."

Notice that there was another rule in the database with picnic(Day) as its head. We can see that this rule would have confirmed tuesday as a day to make potato salad if the Prolog processing had used this rule. Because of the cut, this rule will not be used. The backtracking to the cut will cause the failure of the parent goal

```
picnic(tuesday).
```

and no further attempts at matching will be made.

The cut provides a way of modifying the behavior of Prolog as it processes its goals. The cut is used in conjunction with the other means the programmer has to control behavior; the order in which facts, rules and predicates in rules are written. These control mechanisms have meaning only in the procedural semantics of Prolog. They have no meaning in the declarative semantics.

By modifying the database above, we can gain more insight into how cut affects Prolog's behavior. First, we will add fair weather for the weekend and remove all cuts from the base.

```
holiday(tuesday,july_4).
weather(tuesday,fair).
weather(saturday,fair).
weather(sunday,fair).
weekend(saturday).
weekend(sunday).
make(potato_salad,Day) :- picnic(Day).
picnic(Day) :- weather(Day,fair), weekend(Day).
picnic(Day) :- holiday(Day,july_4).
?- make(potato_salad,When).
When = saturday ;
When = sunday ;
When = tuesday ;
no
```

In this example, most of the backtracking that was done resulted from the user entering a semicolon, asking for more answers. In tracing the goals generated by the query, we can see that only one, early instantiation of When was unsuccessful. Using the first picnic rule, When was instantiated first to tuesday, but then the facts did not meet the requirements for that picnic rule. That rule was used for saturday and sunday. Tuesday was then reported because of the second picnic rule.

To see the effects of cut, we will now modify the first picnic rule to its earlier form.

```
picnic(Day) :- weather(Day,fair), !, weekend(Day).
?- make(potato_salad,When).
no
```

This time we have asked Prolog to give us any instantiation for When rather than asking for confirmation as we did in the first example. Nonetheless, tuesday is the first instantiation made to the variable, When. The backtracking to the cut caused failure of goals clear back to the original

```
make(potato_salad,tuesday).
```

so "no" is reported.

Next, we will modify the first picnic rule so that the cut is furthest right in the body of the rule.

```
picnic(Day) :- weather(Day,fair), weekend(Day), !
?- make(potato_salad,When).
When = saturday ;
no
```

In answering our query this time, Prolog attempted to satisfy the goals in the rule with When instantiated to tuesday as before. This time, however, the goal

```
weekend(tuesday).
```

failed and caused backtracking before the cut was reached. Because the cut had not been activated, Prolog could backtrack and find the new instantiation for When, saturday. The goal

```
picnic(saturday).
```

succeeded through the three subgoals of the rule, including the cut, so Prolog reported

```
When = saturday
```

The semicolon prompt by the user then caused backtracking. Working back from the right in the body of this rule, Prolog encountered the cut. The cut failure caused failure up through the original goal and Prolog reported "no." From this example, we see that Prolog can backtrack among goals to the left of a cut just as though the cut were not there. By the same token, Prolog can backtrack among goals to the right of the cut so long as the cut is not activated by backtracking. That is, we could write the rule

```
picnic(Day) :- !, weather(Day,fair), weekend(Day).
make(potato_salad,When).
When = saturday ;
When = sunday ;
no.
```

In this example, Prolog succeeded in matching all three of the subgoals in the body of the picnic rule and reported

```
When = saturday
```

The semicolon prompt from the user made Prolog backtrack, but only through the two right-most goals. New matches with When instantiated to sunday allowed the goals to succeed so Prolog reported

```
When = sunday
```

The next semicolon prompt, however, forces backtracking to the cut. With cut's failure, the parent goal

```
picnic(When).
```

failed and no more matches were considered.

The overall effect of including a cut as a goal is to force Prolog to limit alternatives. When the cut is activated as a goal, all the choices that have been made since the activation of the parent goal are set. That is, they are treated as if they were the only choice possible. This includes the choice of rules as well as matches and instantiations. Later, when the cut is encountered in backtracking, no other alternatives will be considered for these choices.

EXERCISES 6.3

1. Given this modified database, how will Prolog answer the query?
   ```
   holiday(tuesday,july_4).
   weather(saturday,fair).
   weekend(saturday).
   weekend(sunday).
   make(potato_salad,Day) :- picnic(Day).
   picnic(Day) :- holiday(Day,july_4), !.
   picnic(Day) :- weather(Day,fair), weekend(Day).
   ?- make(potato_salad,When).
   ```
2. How will Prolog respond to the query if the first picnic rule were modified
   ```
   picnic(Day) :- !, holiday(Day,july_4).
   ?- make(potato_salad,When).
   ```
3. Using the rule from Exercise 2 above, what fact could be added to the database to result in a second day being reported to the same query?

6.4 USING CUT

Prolog programmers use cut to limit the backtracking and attempts at resatisfying that their programs do. Eliminating unprofitable searches improves Prolog's efficiency and can make a program more effective. In deciding to use cut, however, the programmer must be aware that these gains may be at the price of the generality of the program.

One specific reason for using cut is to give priority to a specific instantiation of a variable. For example, in the exercises above we saw that the picnic rule with july_4 in it was put first in the multiple picnic rule and the cut was put at its end, Prolog returned only tuesday.

```
picnic(Day) :- holiday(Day,july_4), !.
picnic(Day) :- weather(Day,fair), weekend(Day).
```

The cut in this database effectively changed the meaning of our query from "when can we have a picnic" to "if it's the Fourth of July, of course we'll have the picnic then; forget anything else."

By the same token, in an earlier example we used

```
picnic(Day) :- weather(Day,fair),weekend(Day),!.
```

This can be used to mean "we're not going to picnic both days this weekend; one's enough."

In a similar manner, we can use cut to limit a search when we know there will only be one right answer. In Chapter 5, we saw a rule that processed palindromes

```
palindrome(Half,Whole) :- append(Half,Rest,Whole),
        reverse(Half,Rest).
```

It is clear that if the goal

```
palindrome(Half,Whole).
```

succeeds when it has been given either the Half or the Whole, the only answer has been found. That is,

```
?- palindrome([al,bet],Whole).
Whole = [al,bet,bet,al]
?- palindrome(Half,[ape,bed,bed,ape]).
Half = [ape,bed]
```

Neither of these goals could have another solution. Adding a cut to the definition means that any attempt to resatisfy this goal will fail immediately without further useless searching.

```
palindrome(Half,Whole) :- append(Half,Rest,Whole),
        reverse(Half,Rest), !.
```

The cut is appropriate and useful in these circumstances:
- when there are several parts of a multiple rule that define different criteria for the same conclusion of which only one should be chosen
- when it is known that there will only be one correct answer and further matching attempts are futile.

Both of these uses require that the programmer take a specific view of the role of the program. Adding the cut narrows down the generality of the program segment. For example

```
grandfather(Oldster,Kid) :-
        father(Adult,Kid), !, father(Oldster,Adult).
```

Adding the cut to the rule improves efficiency for searches looking for a grandfather when the Kid is known. The cut forces the end of a search if the Kid's father is found but the father of the father cannot be found. This is effective in the circumstances because individuals (typically) have only one father and there is no sense searching for another.

Fathers, however, often do have more than one child. This rule would not work correctly if the instantiations are going from father to child. Thus the rule can be used effectively to find the grandfather, but not to find the grandchildren.

To see how this works, consider the database and the examples below. The three examples show the rule working (1) correctly, (2) correctly and efficiently, (3) incorrectly because of the particular query.

```
father(garth,lou).
father(garth,sam).
father(sam,tom).
father(sam,joe).
grandfather(Oldster,Kid) :-
        father(Adult,Kid), !, father(Oldster,Adult).

?- grandfather(Old,tom).
        first activate father(Adult,tom).
            succeeds with Adult: sam
        then activate cut, succeeds
        then activate father(Oldster,sam).
            succeeds with Oldster: garth

?- grandfather(Old,lou).
        first activate father(Adult,lou).
            succeeds with Adult: garth
        then activate cut, succeeds
        then activate father(Oldster,garth).
            fails, backtrack over cut
        fail grandfather(Oldster,lou).
```

Note: the search for another match to father(Adult,lou) was not done as it was pointless.

```
?- grandfather(garth,Kid).
        first activate father(Adult,Kid).
            succeeds with Adult: garth and Kid: lou
        then activate cut, succeeds
        then activate father(garth,garth).
            fails, backtrack over the cut
        fail grandfather(garth,Kid).
```

Note: further search would have found matches but the cut prevented them.

Whenever a programmer uses rules that contain cut, he or she should exercise care that the rules will only be asked to carry out the task for which they were designed.

Cut/Fail Combination
Another use of the cut is in combination with a predicate, **fail**. The **fail** predicate is built into the Prolog system and when activated as a goal, immediately fails. Thus, it always causes backtracking.

The **cut/fail** combination is used where there are some instantiations of a predicate that should be eliminated from consideration by a rule. Usually the rule will be a multiple rule that handles a number of different criteria; the expression of the multiple rule can be simplified greatly by eliminating some cases at first. Here is an example based on requirements for having a pet in an apartment building.

```
allow(elephant) :- !,fail.
allow(Animal) :- size(Animal,less_than_50_lb),
        license(Animal).
allow(Animal) :- lives(Animal,cage).
    :
    :
```

The purpose of the first rule in the multiple definition of allow in this example is to remove consideration of elephants at the very start. Because of the **cut/fail** combination, none of the other allow rules will be checked for matching. This provision eliminates even very small elephants that live in cages. It says no elephants need be proposed. A request for elephants may well have failed eventually in the case, perhaps when licensing requirements could not be met, but the **cut/fail** combination yields the "no" promptly.

Negation

The **cut/fail** combination is one way to use negation in a Prolog base. The example above could be paraphrased to

1. If the animal is not an elephant, weighs less than fifty pounds and has a license, it is allowed.
2. If the animal is not an elephant, and lives in a cage, it is allowed.

This use of negation has a powerful effect because the special elephant case need only be entered once, yet it affects use of any of the allow rules. This power has a price: these rules will not work to generate all possible allowed animals, it will only check particular animals.

```
?- allow(What).
no
```

Again, the programmer must be alert to the intended use of a program and if the use changes, all uses of cut must be reconsidered.

Another method of introducing negation to a Prolog program is through a special built-in predicate, **not**. Not is written \+ in some implementations. This negation is quite different in that it can be applied selectively to specific rules. It is important to notice that this negation is also based on a different mechanism. For the goal of

```
not(some_goal).
```

to succeed, the goal, some_goal, must fail in a search through the database.

For example, consider this complete base.

```
order(Vegetable) :- not(green(Vegetable)).
green(beans).
green(broccoli).
green(spinach).

?- order(spinach).
no
```

This answered correctly as spinach, being green, should not be ordered.

```
?- order(cauliflower).
yes
```

This answered correctly as cauliflower, not being green, should be ordered.

```
?- order(collard_greens).
yes
```

This is not correct from our view; collard greens are green. The problem is that Prolog did not have a fact that says collard greens are green, so by the closed world assumption, they could not be. By the same token, a query with a variable will not work. The variable will be instantiated in the first match it makes, causing the match to succeed and the not to fail. This will be the case even if references to other vegetables appear further in the database. In a Prolog program not(some_goal) is true if some_goal fails within the base.

EXERCISES 6.4

1. If **not** were not a built-in predicate, an equivalent could be written using **cut/fail**. Write a rule in place of
   ```
   order(Vegetable).
   ```
   from above that replaces the **not**. It will require two rules.
2. There is a built-in predicate, **call**, which activates whatever predicate is given as its argument. Thus
   ```
   call(some_goal)
   ```
   activates the goal, some_goal. The **call** goal succeeds if the goal, some_goal, succeeds. Write a pair of rules with head
   ```
   isnt(some_goal)
   ```
   that works the same way as the **not** predicate described above.

6.5 RULES OF THUMB FOR CUT
The purpose in using cut in a Prolog program is to modify the processing pattern Prolog will use. As we have discussed, the cut can be used to give some conditions priority over others and to save some time and work on Prolog's part. These uses of the cut typically limit Prolog to checking facts rather than generating possible variable instantiations.

Cut is also used to make a recursive rule workable that, when generating variable instantiations, would go on infinitely. The cut is not used in this manner to "fix" an uncontrolled recursion. Rather, there are certain problems whose solutions require generation of an unknown number of possibilities before the desired choice is found. For example, you may be searching through a class roster, looking for a student who earned 100% on an exam. As soon as you find one, you will stop looking. For this kind of problem, the Prolog program may use the cut as a stopping condition.

Using cut sometimes makes a Prolog program harder to read and understand. A cut construct can often be eliminated by using **not** instead, which makes the program easier to read. In other cases, however, the cut is necessary for controlling processing.

SUMMARY

Any Prolog program can be considered descriptively (as a definition) and also prescriptively (as a procedure). The Prolog programmer must consider pragmatic matters in the Prolog system as well as the logical correctness of the program.

The programmer exerts control over processing by arranging rules and facts in a particular order or by using special predicates, particularly *cut*, to control the Prolog search pattern.

Descriptive Semantics	Prescriptive Semantics
Declarative	Procedural
Definitions	Directions
Logic	Control
Completeness/correctness	Efficiency
Analysis of problem	Process of solution
World-definition	Set of directions
What is done	How it is done

EXERCISES CHAPTER 6 ▮▮▮▮▮▮▮▮▮▮▮▮▮▮▮▮▮▮▮▮▮▮

1. Identify the Prolog concept or concepts described by each phrase below.
    a) Two ways to view a Prolog program.
    b) These can be satisfied and resatisfied.
    c) Two concerns that we can consider separately when writing a Prolog program.
    d) Stepping back to a decision point to make a new choice.
    e) A built-in predicate that cuts off alternative choices.
    f) The group of rules that share the same predicate in their head.
    g) In the descriptive view of Prolog, the way facts and rules are treated.
    h) In the prescriptive view of Prolog, the way facts and rules are treated.

2 Using the Prolog database given below, diagram the goals/subgoals and the processing path for the question.

```
flower(roses,red).
flower(violets,blue).
clothes(hat,blue).
clothes(coat,white).
?- flowers(What,Color),clothes(Which,Color).
```

3. a) Given this database and query, Prolog responds no. Explain the processing that results in this response.

```
allow(elephant) :- !, fail.
allow(Animal) :- lives(Animal,cage).
lives(boa,cage).
?- allow(What).
```

   b) If the database were rearranged, how and why would the question be answered now.

```
allow(Animal) :- lives(Animal,cage).
allow(elephant) :- !, fail.
lives(boa,cage).
?- allow(What).
```

4. Write a Prolog program of rules for a diet, specifying food items that are acceptable for eating. Include rules for at least three items that are not acceptable, and put rules to exclude them first in the database.

Using Built-in Predicates

The purpose of this chapter is to help the learner:
- be aware of many of the predicates that are commonly available across a number of Prolog implementations.
- understand a conceptual grouping of built-in predicates for
  facilitating reference.
  understanding roles.

7.1 ROLES OF BUILT-IN PREDICATES
As part of every Prolog system, certain capabilities will be provided. A few of these capabilities are part of the Prolog structure. For example, the prompts (?-) and the organization of the database are designed into the software that is in control of the Prolog environment. These capabilities are necessary so that we can actually use Prolog in conjunction with a computer system.

Other capabilities are made available to the programmer are through built-in predicates. These predicates are used just like the predicates that the Prolog programmer designs. They are, however, available for use without the need for definition. Exactly which predicates are built-in differs from system to system. Each programmer should check the manual for the Prolog system being used to be sure which predicates are built-in on that system.

Many of the built-in predicates are simply for convenience. They are predicates that the programmer could build from the other tools available, but since they are commonly used, special provision is made for them. For example, **nl**, which moves output to a "new line" could be written with **put** and the ASCII codes for return and line feed. Using **nl** is much more convenient.

Other built-in predicates are needed because they do tasks that are not possible in the pure Prolog model. Input and output control are examples of these kinds of predicates. The Prolog model, having a set of facts and rules of which questions are asked, has no place for interaction with a universe outside the world that the database defines. Any action on the part of the Prolog program that goes beyond pattern-matching and variable instantiation is outside pure Prolog. These actions are called *side-effects* of the predicates.

The predicates typically built-in to a Prolog system can be grouped according to the kind of task they are designed to do. These roles include
- building and modifying databases,
- input and output of questions and answers,
- modification of processing pattern (control),
- doing arithmetic,
- observing and debugging processing,
- building data objects,
- manipulating terms.

In addition to providing information on specific predicates, this chapter is designed to provide the reader with some structure within which to organize the predicates. Input and output, modification of processing, doing arithmetic and tracing are all discussed in greater detail in other chapters in this book. They are included here because this chapter addresses the grouping of predicates. Understanding this organization of predicates makes it easier to choose the appropriate predicates for the task at hand.

Building and Modifying Databases
The creation of a correct, complete database is the central goal for the Prolog programmer. The database contains the definitions of all rules and facts, all the assertions from which information can be derived. The database describes a closed world which Prolog assumes is complete and consistent. To use the Prolog world, the programmer enters the assertions into the database in the computer.

Most typically, the assertions will be written into a computer file for ongoing storage. From the file, they must be transferred to the database. The two built-in predicates for this role are **consult**, which adds contents of a file to the database, and **reconsult**, which adds new assertions and replaces old ones in the base. The assertions that are replaced are those that have the same predicate name and number of arguments as the new assertions in the reconsulted file. One can **consult** or **reconsult** the user, which allows assertions to be added to the database by typing them at the user's terminal.

Individual assertions can be added by using the **assert** predicates. Either facts or rules can be added; rules require an extra set of parentheses. Because the order in which assertions appear in the database affects Prolog's processing, two **assert** forms are available: **asserta** which enters a new assertion before any others with the same predicate and **assertz** which enters the new assertion after any current assertions with the same predicate.

For example: `asserta(green(cheese)).`
`assertz((taste(exotic) :- green(cheese))).`

In a like manner, assertions can be removed from the database. **Retract** removes the assertion specified and **abolish** removes all assertions with a predicate and arity that match the specification.

For example: `retract(green(cheese)).`
`abolish(taste,1).`

The **assert** and **retract** predicates can be used in conjunction with predicates that get input during processing, like **read** (see next section), or with predicates that manipulate terms like **functor** (see Manipulating Terms and Variables below).

This ability to manipulate the database is one of the reasons Prolog is a good language to apply to complex problems or problems that are not clearly understood. As the problem becomes better understood or special cases are isolated, the Prolog database can be modified to meet the new requirements.

Input and Output of Questions and Answers

In the Prolog model, the database is the description of a world. To explore the world or derive information from it, we ask questions and receive answers. The question and answer communication is our interaction with Prolog. Unless we specify some other source and receiver for the questioning/answering, the interaction is with the user. In cases where we want to modify the standard question/answer interaction, we need to use predicates that handle input and output.

There are two reasons to modify the interaction. The first is to modify the form of the interaction. The basic Prolog interaction is terse and assumes the user needs no information beyond the standard prompt, ?- and the assertion-based answers. If the user is someone not familiar with the program, more information in the interaction is helpful. Even if the user is familiar with the program (say is the programmer) more information may facilitate the use.

The second reason for modifying the interaction is to allow the source of questions or receiver of answers to be a file rather than the user. A file is a more appropriate source when the question that is to be processed is long or complex (for example, a paragraph to be searched for keywords). A file is also a good choice for results that we need to retain after the Prolog interaction is over.

The idea underlying Prolog's input and output is the stream. Input comes from the input stream and output goes to the output stream. If no other is specified, both streams are assigned to the user's terminal. Other streams are specified using a set of predicates, the **see** predicates for modifying the input stream and the **tell** predicates for output.

Whatever streams are being used, pieces of data are accessed in the input stream and placed in the output stream using a group of built-in predicates. The pieces of data can be handled in two ways: a character at a time or a term at a time.

If each character is going to be handled individually, then predicates of the **get** and **put** family are used. For terms (a constant, a variable or a structure) **read** and **write** are used. Examples of programs that control input and output are in Chapter 8. Appendix E lists syntax rules for these predicates and a number of related predicates in the form they appear in DECsystem-10/20 Prolog. Because input, output and file manipulation require coordination with parts of the computer system outside Prolog proper, system-specific problems often arise. The programmer should be alert to the possibility and check the system manual for specifics.

Processing Control

Some special symbols we have been using since the beginning of the book communicate to Prolog about processing. The comma in conjunctions, the semi-colon and the period at the end of clauses, give specific signals to Prolog's control mechanism. Similarly, **not** and the cut, **!**, modify Prolog's standard control process. These, along with the **cut/fail** combination are discussed in Chapter 6.

Fail is a predicate that can be used in other roles in addition to the **cut/fail** combination. Since **fail** always fails when it is activated as a goal, it always causes backtracking. That means that if we have a predicate that we want to reactivate, we can follow it by **fail**. Say we wanted to write all the values for an argument in a set of facts in our database about the week's weather, a goal that would accomplish it is

```
?- weather(Day,Outlook), write(Outlook), fail.
```

Each time weather succeeds, **write** will succeed, doing output of the value, then **fail** will cause backtracking. **Write**, being an input/output predicate, cannot be resatisfied, so backtracking goes to weather. Weather can be resatisfied, so the process starts again. It will repeat until the weather finally exhausts all possibilities, whereupon the goal fails. In the meanwhile, however, all the values for Outlook have been printed.

Another method for creating repetition is the predicate **repeat**. The **repeat** predicate, when first encountered in processing, simply succeeds. When backtracking returns to the **repeat** predicate, processing begins again just as it did at the first success of the repeat goal. The repeat will continue generalizing new cycles through the process as long as it is backtracked to. To stop the repetition process, backtracking must be stopped. That means that the special case for stopping will succeed instead of fail. For example, this rule reads terms from the user until the word "stop" is reached.

```
eat_words :- repeat, read(Item), check(Item), !.
check(stop) :- !.
check(Value) :- fail.
```

In the fundamental Prolog model, recursion provides the facility for causing repetition. **Repeat** and **fail** are predicates for repetition that use a different underlying plan. Recursion can be viewed as the jointed telescope from Chapter 5, where important work is being done both on the way into the problem (left-to-right) and on the way out (right-to-left). The repetition of **repeat** and **fail** is more like stroking a cat; the useful work is only one way.

Observing and Debugging Processing

We have already seen several predicates for observing Prolog's processing. There are three reasons to observe processing:
- to learn how Prolog works.
- to see how a process is carried out with an eye toward making changes to improve efficiency.
- to find bugs that prevent correct processing.

We can observe processing at different levels. The **log** predicate records a copy of the programmer interaction. The **listing** predicate shows the current content of the database. The **trace** predicate displays the succession of goal activations and matches. **Trace** is actually one part of the **debug** predicate which also has other components. For example, with one option in **debug**, a particular goal can be specified and then whenever that goal is activated, it will be reported to the user.

Additional predicates that are useful in observing and debugging are **ancestors** and **subgoal_of**. Ancestors creates (or tests) a list of the goals that were activated for the current goal. **Subgoal_of** succeeds if the current goal is a subgoal of the goal specified as an argument in the predicate. These predicates can be used to discover and display what is effectively a path through the diagrams of processing that we looked at in Section 6.1.

Arithmetic Manipulations

Understanding the built-in predicates for using Prolog to do arithmetic requires a clear understanding of the difference between an arithmetic expression and an arithmetic value. An arithmetic expression is a sequence of one or more symbols that represent arithmetic operators or arithmetic values. For example:

```
X + Y
2 + 3
X - 4
```

Within expressions, variables can represent other expressions. That is, in the examples, X and Y could be expressions themselves. Expressions have no value unless they are evaluated by the use of one of the predicates that specifically causes evaluation. Before an expression can be evaluated, any variables in the expression must be instantiated to integer values.

The arithmetic operators, like + and −, are predicates, but they do not cause evaluation. The predicates for comparing two expressions do cause evaluation. For example <, which is read "is less than," causes evaluation of the two expressions with it. For example

```
X + 2 < Y - 1
```

When this goal is activated, X and Y must have values so that the expressions can be evaluated. If, after evaluation, the first expression value is less than the second, this goal will succeed. Such a goal could appear in a rule:

```
correct_pair :- get(X), get(Y), X + 2 < Y - 1.
```

The syntax of the arithmetic goal looks much different from most goals we have seen. The rule could be written

```
correct_pair :- get(X), get(Y), <(+(X,2), -(Y,1)).
```

Because most people are more familiar with arithmetic forms like the first example, Prolog has special facility to allow that form. A predicate that evaluates an expression and instantiates a variable to that value is **is**. For example, the goal

```
Square is X * X.
```

instantiates Square to the square of X. When **is** is called, X must have a value so the expression can be evaluated.

Among the predicates is one that tests two values to see if they are equal. It is written **=:=**. In the next two sections, we will see two other predicates for "equal" that have different roles. A comparison of the three is made in Section 7.3.

Manipulating Terms and Variables

In Prolog, we have the facility to get information defining an object from outside the database and then to move the object into the database, making it part of the world with which we are working. If the object is something we know about we can put it in directly. It is more powerful, though, to build an object during Prolog processing and then add it to the world as an assertion. In this way, our world can "learn" from its interaction of questions and answers. Since we will need a general form for this activity, we will use variables to represent the new assertions we are building. Building new assertions generally requires use of several built-in predicates in conjunction. For example, this rule will read in three terms and turn them into an assertion.

```
new_fact :- read(A1), read(A2), read(A3),
      functor(C,A3,2),
      arg(1,C,A1),
      arg(2,C,A2),
      assert(C).
```

The rule first reads in three terms as variables. (In a real program, getting these terms might be more complex.) Then **functor** sets up a pattern for the structure. The structure is named C, has A3 for its predicate and has two arguments. The two **arg** predicates instantiate A1 and A2 as arguments one and two in the structure, then **assert** actually puts the structure into the database.

If the structure being manipulated is in a list instead of being separate terms then **=..** (pronounced univ) is used to transform the object from a list to a predicate and arguments or back. Similarly, **name** transforms atoms or integers to and from a list of codes for letters and numbers. The predicates that modify the Prolog database, particularly **univ**, **functor** and **arg**, are used frequently in programs that build their own world description. For example, a program that is gathering information about a science experiment could use **functor** and **arg** to enter facts about the experiment into the database.

If instead of putting a clause into the database as an assertion, we want to activate a goal that has been created as a variable, we can use the predicate **call**. By changing the last component of new__fact to the goal,

```
call(C).
```

we will cause the structure that we just built to become the current active goal.

While manipulating these objects as variables, we may need to check on the values, either their characteristics (is this an integer?) or their instantiated values. The two tests, == for equal and \ == for not equal, check the instantiated values on a literal (character by character) basis. For example

```
?- color(green) == color(green).
yes
?- color(X) == color(X).
X = _23
yes
?- color(green) == color(X).
no
?- color(X) == color(Y).
no
```

EXERCISES 7.1

1. Programs with a lot of input and output tend to be explained procedurally rather than descriptively. Why?
2. Indicate whether the following queries will succeed or fail.
   ```
   ?- A==A.
   ?- A==a.
   ?- A=:=a.
   ?- weather(today)==weather(today).
   ?- weather(today)==weather(When).
   ?- weather(When)==weather(When).
   ?- weather(today)==weather(friday).
   ```

7.2 Building Data Objects

There are several predicates that create objects or lists of objects by analyzing Prolog elements for their parts. These transfer instantiations or information about instantiations from one object to another. The object may be a simple object, like a constant, or an aggregate object, like a list or structure. The data objects that are built act as intermediate gathering or storage places for elements that will have more processing done with them.

One predicate is =. Say a goal is activated like this:

Prolog tries to make a match with the terms X and Y. In the process, it will-instantiate as many variables in X and Y as necessary. If they can be matched the goal succeeds; otherwise it fails. As a result of the matching, copies of objects can be made.

```
?- this(one) = this(one).
    yes
?- this(one) = this(One).
    One = one
    yes
?- this(one) = this(two).
    no
?- this(one,also) = this(What,also).
    What = one
    yes
?- this(One,also) = this(Two,also).
    One = _24
    Two = _24
    yes
```

Here a match can be made because the "this" functor matches, both terms have two components, the "also" part matches, and One and Two are both uninstantiated variables so they can be made to match. In this case, they can be made to match by associating both One and Two with __24. The internal form for the variable, an underscore-integer, is reported.

```
?- this(One,also) = this(two,Why).
    One = two
    Why = also
    yes
?- line([one,Two,three]) = line([One,two,three]).
    Two = two
    One = one
    yes
```

Another predicate that creates a value is **length** which finds the length of a list. It has two arguments, the list and the integer representing the number of elements in the list. If the first is instantiated to a list, the second will be instantiated to its length.

```
?- length([a,b,c],S).
S = 3
yes
?- length([a,b,c],2).
no
?- a(L) = a([a,b]),length(L,S).
L = [a,b]
S = 2
yes
```

If the first argument is not instantiated to a specific list, an error will be reported.

A predicate that builds a new list based on an existing one is **sort**. The elements of the list in the first argument are sorted into order and the new list is instantiated to the second argument. Duplicate values are eliminated from the list.

```
?- sort([b,c,a],L2).
    L2 = [a,b,c]
    yes
?- sort([a,a,c,b],L2).
    L2 = [a,b,c]
    yes
?- sort([16,12,32],L2).
    L2 = [12,16,32]
    yes
```

The **sort** predicate is not symmetric. The first argument must be instantiated when **sort** is activated.

```
?- sort(L1,[a,b]).
**Error: length(_24)
no
```

Two predicates that gather instances of occurrence of objects are **bagof** and **setof**. To use these predicates, we specify a goal and a variable in the goal. The predicates search through the database to find all appearances of the goal that can be proved true. For each true goal, the constant value that was instantiated to the specified variable is gathered into the bag. The bag (a list) is instantiated to the variable given in the third argument of the predicate. If there are no occurrences, the goal fails. This database and query using the **bagof** predicate show how to collect a list of constants designated by the variable.

```
parent(jan,bet).
parent(jan,cat).
parent(joe,ann).
parent(joe,cat).
?- bagof(Child,parent(jan,Child),B).
B = [bet,cat]
yes
```

If there is more than one possible list of instances because of another variable in the specified goal, the goal can backtrack and find other responses. For example, given

```
parent(jan,bet).
parent(jan,cat).
parent(joe,ann).
parent(joe,cat).
?- bagof(Child,parent(Who,Child),B).
Who = jan   B = [bet,cat] ;
Who = joe   B = [ann,cat] ;
no
```

The instantiation of different bags can be gathered into a single response by using what is called an existential quantifier on the non-gathered variables from the goal. The variable name followed by a caret (^) appears just before the predicate. A predicate with several variables requires a sequence (e.g., A^B^C^D^).

Using the database above

```
?- bagof(Child,Who^(parent(Who,Child)),B).
B = [bet,cat,ann,cat]
Who = _45
Child = _24 ;
no
```

This existential quantifier (read X^ as "there is an X such that") is used only in **bagof** and **setof**.

The **setof** predicate works as though **bagof** is used to gather the values into a list before the list is sorted. As in the result of **sort**, any duplicates will have been removed.

Using the database from above

```
?- setof(Child,P^(parent(P,Child)),S),
    S = [ann,bet,cat]
    P = _45
    Child = _24 ;
    no
```

▇ EXERCISES 7.2

1. Assuming facts about a week's weather of the form
   weather(<day>,<outlook>).
   write a rule that will gather a list of days with similar outlook on the weather.
2. Write a rule as above that lists all seven of the days' outlooks.
3. Write a rule as above that list the variety of weather throughout the week (no duplicates in entries).
4. Write a rule that reports how many different kinds of weather there were over the week.

7.3 PREDICATES IN THE SYSTEM
In earlier sections of this chapter, we saw three different predicates that represent the relationship of equality. The first **=:=** is for equality of arithmetic values. It is used with two expressions that can be evaluated (they have no uninstantiated variables). Its activation cannot therefore cause the instantiation

of any variables. It has a negative form, so that "not equal" can succeed. The second == is for literal equality of two terms. That is, the terms must be exactly alike in their functors, arguments and organization. Thus

```
X + 2 == X + 2  — succeeds literally
X + 2 =:= X + 2 — fails if X not instantiated
                — succeeds if X is instantiated
```

The literal equality test also has a negative form so "not equal" can succeed in appropriate cases. These literally equal predicates also do not instantiate any variables. Two uninstantiated variables will only be considered literally equal if they have previously been designated equal.

The third equality predicate = is the least stringent of the three. It can be used to test general equality of objects including numbers, constants, variables, and lists. If there are any uninstantiated variables in the objects being equated, those variables will be instantiated to matching. Thus

```
cheese(green) = cheese(X)
```

will instantiate X to green

```
cheese(X) = cheese(Y)
```

will designate X and Y to be the same variable internally. As a result

```
cheese(X) = cheese(Y), X == Y
```

will succeed. The "not equal" form of =, which is \=, is less commonly built-in to Prolog's than are the other "not equal" forms.

Predicate	Use	Instantiates Variables
=:=	arithmetic values	no
==	literal structures	no
=	any objects	yes

The large number of predicates built into the typical Prolog system complicate the programming process while they facilitate it. Almost all the built-in predicates represent an extension of the central idea of a world from which inquiries are made. Most testing for equality, for example, is done through Prolog's pattern matching, not through using built-in predicates.

SUMMARY

Every Prolog implementation has built-in facilities for the programmer to use. Built-in predicates in some cases are just for the programmers convenience. In other cases, they handle tasks, such as input and output that are outside the pure Prolog model of success of goals within a defined database.

Built-in predicates fall into categories according to the roles they serve. Those roles are:
- building and modifying databases,
- input and output of questions and answers,
- modification of processing pattern (control),
- doing arithmetic,
- observing and debugging processing,
- building data objects,
- manipulating terms.

The programmer who understands the task to be done can use this organization to look for the appropriate predicate to facilitate programming that task.

EXERCISES CHAPTER 7

1. Indicate which of the following will succeed and which will fail.
   ```
   ?- X = a, Y = a, X == Y.
   ?- X = a, Y = a, X = Y.
   ?- X = a, Y = a, X =:= Y.
   ?- X = Y, X == Y.
   ?- X = Y, X = Y.
   ?- X = Y, X =:= Y.
   ```
2. In this chapter, seven roles of built-in predicates are listed. For each role, specify a programming problem that will require using a built-in predicate from that group.
3. Write Prolog programs for these problems.
   a) Go through a data base of facts of the form
   ```
   made_of(<fruit>,<product>).
   ```
   to find all the products made of each fruit.
   b) Use the same database to find an alphabetized list of products for each fruit.
   c) Use the same database to find an alphabetized list of products for all fruit together.
   d) Use the database to determine how many different products are made from fruit.

Input, Output and the Environment

The purpose of this chapter is to help the learner:
- understand the general workings of the Prolog programming environment.
- create and modify databases using files, interaction and predicates.
- read and write using various input/output streams.
- do character input/output.
- consider some facets of building a user interface.

8.1 PROGRAMMING ENVIRONMENT

An environment is something that surrounds us. It affects the way we do things by providing mechanisms for carrying out tasks. A programming environment includes ways to create programs, use programs, store the programs and results, and observe the execution of programs.

Characteristics of programming environments differ on different computer systems and for different programming languages. Some environments are much more helpful and convenient than others, especially in the areas of storage and of observing what the computer, under control of the program, is doing. This process of observing behavior is available in most Prolog environments, usually under the name "trace." Tracing is a useful tool for discovering and correcting errors (called debugging). The user manuals for a particular system will have details of how to trace programs in that system's Prolog environment.

The process of creating, modifying and storing programs in the Prolog environment uses two levels of mechanisms. The first level is provided through the master program (also called the supervisor) which is part of the computer system. This program keeps track of storage, provides printouts, and generally runs the computer system including coordination for the Prolog-specific activity. At the next level, the Prolog-specific activity, another program carries out the main task of the machine doing Prolog: to accept a predicate and see if the predicate is consistent with the database.

This, of course, is not a trivial task. The predicate may be one that the programmer has entered, in which case Prolog's task is based on the things we have discussed in Chapters 2–6 in this book. The predicate may also be one of the *built-in predicates*, predicates that have been provided by the people who wrote the program that does Prolog. Built-in predicates are discussed in Chapter 7 and Appendix E, but a few of them are also discussed here, as they deal with the Prolog programming environment. These predicates have a more imperative flavor about them than most predicates. That is, they are more like commands than relationships. For example, **listing**, which displays the database to the user, is a built-in predicate. These predicates are used both in managing the databases and in handling the questions and answers that are part of Prolog programs.

Managing Databases

One way to create and modify databases in Prolog is *interactively*, using the keyboard to type facts and rules into the database. To do this, we first type *[user]*. Then any items typed in go into the database until we type control-Z. The square-bracket notation is actually shorthand for a built-in predicate **consult**.

```
?- consult(user).
```

This works because the user, the person at the keyboard, is the source of the facts and rules. Being consulted means acting as the source of the data for the base. The argument for the **consult** predicate is properly a *file name*.

```
?- consult(<filename>).
```

A file is a collection of pieces of data. In computing, files are created, stored, printed out and accessed. They are thought of to some degree as physical objects even though they actually are collections of pieces of data. Thus, when the user is being treated as a file, he or she is not being equated with a folder in a file cabinet. Rather, the user is acting as a source of information. Files have names associated with them so that they can be kept track of and accessed. The Prolog programmer usually builds and modifies files using an editor, a piece of software separate from Prolog. An editor's purpose is creating and modifying files; editors do that task better than Prolog does.

One problem with using [user] to build Prolog databases is that saving the database to use again often has problems. While most systems have a command (like **save**(<name>)) to save the current database, the form in which it is saved is often difficult to manipulate. An independently built and stored file is more convenient. Prolog programmers often combine these two sources of database information when developing or testing a program. They consult a file for the base, then interactively add or remove particular facts or rules. Any changes decided on should be noted and later changed in the file using the editor.

There are several mechanisms for interactively modifying a database. One can **consult** a second file. This adds all the contents of the second file to the database already there. One can also **reconsult** a file.

```
reconsult(<filename>).
```

Reconsulting puts new facts and rules into the database, just as **consult** does. The difference is that **reconsult** replaces rules and facts that are already in the database wherever the predicate is the same. Thus **consult** adds to the definition of a rule and **reconsult** replaces it if a new definition is given.

If a programmer wanted, for example, to experiment with the picnic database that was used as an example of the predicate, **cut**, he or she could **consult** the file that had the facts and various rules, including the two

```
picnic(Day) :- weather(Day,fair), !, weekend(Day)
picnic(Day) :- holiday(Day,july_4).
```

After asking the database some questions and observing Prolog's behavior, the programmer could **reconsult** another file that contained only the rules

```
picnic(Day) :- holiday(Day,july_4), !.
picnic(Day) :- weather(Day,fair), weekend(Day).
```

Reconsulting replaces the picnic rules with the new rules and leaves the rest of the database as it was.

Like consulting, reconsulting has a shorthand notation, square brackets with a hyphen before the file name

```
[-second].
```

Consulting several files and reconsulting can be combined.

```
[picnic,-second].
```

Generally, if a file has a special character in its name (and on some systems always) the file name must be enclosed in single quote marks.

```
['picnic.one',-'picnic.two'].
```

Consult and **reconsult** are built-in predicates so the user keys them in like any predicate in response to the **?-** prompt. Prolog processes them and returns a "yes."

There is another group of predicates that add or remove items in the database. These are **assert**, of which there are several forms, and **retract** (or **abolish**). Chapter 7 has more detail about these specific predicates and their forms are shown in Appendix E. There is variation from system to system on many of these predicates, so the particular system manual is the most dependable source of specific information.

We have been considering these predicates for use in interactive communication with Prolog. They can also be used as part of the Prolog database, providing a mechanism for a program to change itself. For example, here is a log of a Prolog interaction.

```
?- listing.
check_again :- assert(today(monday)).
yes
?- today(monday).
no
?- check_again.
yes
?- today(monday).
yes
?- listing.
check_again :- assert(today(monday)).
today(monday)
yes
?-
```

In this example, the activation of the goal, check__again, caused the fact to be added to the base. Rules can be added in the same way, but should be enclosed in an extra set of parentheses in the **assert** argument. For example, the query below will add the blue sky rule to the database.

```
?- assert((sky(blue) :- weather(fair))).
```

1. Write a rule that, when activated, replaces itself with a new rule from a file.
2. Write a database of three rules in which calling on any rule eliminates that rule.
3. Write a database that will give this interaction.

```
?- same(up,down).
yes
?- not(same(up,down))
yes
```

8.2 QUESTIONS AND ANSWERS

In addition to the database, a Prolog program depends on queries to carry out its work. The question/answer process is the dynamic driver that makes Prolog useful. Questions can be included in files that are consulted. When Prolog encounters them, they are activated and succeed or fail as usual. Most commonly, though, questions come from the user. Interacting with Prolog, the user provides the questions and receives the answers. The user is acting again as a file, a source of data items.

As a generalization in computing, a source of items for a computer to process is called an *input stream* and the place where results of the processing are going is called the *output stream*. In Prolog the user is the *default* file for both the input stream and the output stream. Default simply means the choice a computer system will make if it has not been given any other directions.

Sometimes other files for input and output are better than the default user interaction. For input, there may be a number of questions to be asked many times, or the questions may be difficult to type without errors. For output, it may be helpful to have a record of the answers or results of the process for further use later. Prolog has mechanisms, again built-in predicates, to allow use of specified files for either the input or output stream.

For input, the system first must be told which file to use as the input stream. This is done with the predicate, **see**.

```
see(<filename>).
```

This *opens* the file for accessing items. To get a specific item, we can use any of several built-in predicates. Getting a piece of data as input is called *reading* from the file. When a file is opened with **see**, reading always begins at the beginning of the file.

One predicate to access an item is **read**.

```
read(Item).
```

The item will include a clause (the letters and characters) through the termi-
nator, a period. The item must also have a blank or return in the file after it.
For example, say we had the file, star, containing

```
today(friday).
```

and the current database is

```
do_this :- see(star), read(Item),
      assert(Item), seen.
```

This rule says that do_this consists of opening star to read, reading an item,
asserting that item, then closing star as the input stream. The period at the
end of the clause in the file is not carried along, but **assert** adds one in the
database. A Prolog interaction using do_this would look like this.

```
?- do_this.
yes
?- listing.
do_this :- see(star), read(Item),
      assert(Item), seen.
today(friday).
yes
?-
```

At this point, the file, star, is closed and input is not available from it any
longer. This resulted from using the predicate, **seen**, which does not have an
argument. Since the input file has been closed, the input stream reverts to the
default value, user. Notice that only one stream is available to read from at
any one time. (The only exception to this: the added commands of the **tty**
family allow input from the user terminal while another file is the input
stream. See Appendix E.)

Read can also be used to check that a value from a file matches a value in
the database. Assume the contents of star as

```
today(friday).
help.
   :
```

and

```
do_this_one :- see(star), read(Item),
      read(help), seen.
```

When the Prolog user keys in

```
do_this_one.
yes
?-
```

Prolog read the first item in the file and instantiated it to Item as before, then the next **read**, because it has a constant value, checked to see if the values matched. Since they did, the goal succeeded.

Had we used a different rule

```
try_this :- see(star), read(Item),
       read(harp), seen.
```

Not only would the goal, try_this, not have succeeded, but in its failure to match in the second **read**, it will cause a further problem. The problem arises because these input predicates can only succeed once; they cannot be back-tracked to and resatisfied. Meanwhile the input stream has been set to the file and the Prolog system cannot proceed with directives from the user. Input predicates have characteristics such as these that make them different from other Prolog predicates. This is because manipulating input and output is not integral to the Prolog model. Programmers, however, often do want to mani-pulate input and output, so these predicates are provided within the system.

When a previously prepared file is the input stream, the programmer usually wants to process the whole file. The file will always have some special marker, to mark the end of the file. The Prolog program then can process until it reaches the *end of file marker*. This facility allows variation in file length. As an example of a way to process to the end of the file, we will use the predicate, **repeat**, which provides an unending series of new choices on backtracking. The processing of any Item except the end_of_file causes backtracking. The end_of_file Item lets process succeed so the procedure do_file can be finished. The final **cut** prevents redoing of do_file.

```
do_file(Name) :- see(Name),
       repeat,
       read(Item),
       process(Item),
       seen,
       !.
process(Item) :- end_of_file(Item), !
process(Item) :- ...,fail.
```

We also need a definition for the end of file test. The end of file marker varies from system to system and is even called by different names in different parts of the same system. Control-Z is common (e.g. for end of [user]). In other systems the directive "end" marks the end of the file. In the program above, the fact to be matched might look like

```
end_of_file(:- end).
```

In a manner similar to the input, the output stream can be directed to a file. The predicate, **tell** is used to open a file and **told**, which has no argument, closes the file. Sending the output to a file is called *writing* the file. If the output file already contains some data, it is lost when the new data is written. When **told** is activated, an end_of_file marker is entered in the file. Like input, only one output stream is available at one time, except for the user terminal (using **tty** predicates).

The following program copies one file into another. Its processing control is much like the procedure above. Prepare opens the files and shut_files closes them. The main control is embedded in the process predicate. **Repeat** generates repeated starts on the read and handle pair. As long as the Item is not the end_of_file, the Item is written to the new file (and followed by a period to mark the end of the term) then **fail** causes backtracking to the **repeat**. The end_of_file allows process to succeed and copy to be completed.

For writing, another predicate is used here. It is **nl**, which stands for new line. Items in the file must, as before, end with a period and have a blank (or "return") following them.

```
copy(In,Out) :- prepare(In,Out).
     process, shut_files, !.
end_of_file(:- end).
prepare(A,B) :- see(A), tell(B)
shut_files :- seen,told.
process :- repeat, read(Item), handle(Item).
handle(Item) :- end_of_file(Item),!.
handle(Item) :- write(Item), write('.'), nl, fail.
```

EXERCISES 8.2

1. Write a program that reads a question out of a file, processes the question in the current database, then reports its success or failure to the user.
2. Design the contents of a file so that, when consulted, it reads an item from a second file. This item would be the name of a third file which should then be consulted.

8.3 BUILDING A USER INTERFACE

In addition to using files for input and output, the Prolog programmer may want to exert influence over the way input is accepted and output is provided to the program user. The communication between the computer and the program user is called an *interface*.

For example, to go to our earlier database about a week's weather.

```
weather(sunday,fair).
weather(monday,cloudy).
    .
    .
    .
```

The user could inquire about a day's weather by asking in predicate form

```
?- weather(monday,What).
```

It would be easier, especially for the naive user, to have Prolog ask:

```
What day's weather do you want?
```

and have the user type in:

```
monday
```

There are two different components involved in building the structure for an interface

1. reading and writing to "user" as a file
2. manipulating text as characters rather than in Prolog's units, (e.g. list elements).

There is another important component, the natural language interpretation, that will not be considered here. That is, if a user responds

```
first of the week
```

to a request for a day, another whole semantic process would be needed to interpret that phrase into a specific day of the week so that the database could be used to find the response.

To read from the user or write to the user, the same predicates are used as are used for any file. If no other file has been specified for the input or output stream, the user fills both these roles. The user is the only file that can be both input and output streams at the same time.

One way to write output that looks like a usual sentence is to put words in a list, then write the elements of the list successively. A multiple rule that recursively processes a list can be defined.

```
show([ ]) :- nl.
show([Head|Tail]) :- write(Head), tab(1), show(Tail).
```

The new predicate, **tab**, provides spaces between elements. Its argument is an integer, the number of spaces.

If we use this definition on a list,

```
show([what,days,weather,do,you,want]).
```

the output on the user's screen would be

```
what days weather do you want
```

To improve this, we would like a capital letter on the first word and some punctuation in this sentence. However, a capital letter turns the word, What, into a variable, which would then be written by our procedure in the variable form, an underscore-number. Similarly, some punctuation characters have other meaning to Prolog. We can override these special uses by putting single quote marks around the elements that could be confused. Putting single quotes around 'What' prevents its interpretation as a variable, quotes around 'want?' make the question mark an unspecial character and the four single quotes in 'day''s' signals that we actually want one quote mark in the word. Thus

```
show (['What','day''s',weather,do,you,'want?']).
```

will appear on the screen as

```
What day's weather do you want?
```

Given the content below in a database, a typical user interaction would be like that which follows.

```
weather(sunday,fair).
weather(monday,cloudy).
weather(tuesday,fair).
weather(wednesday,fair).
weather(thursday,cloudy).
weather(friday,rainy).
weather(saturday,fair).
process(What) :-
     show(['What','day''s',weather,do,you,'want? ']),
     read(Day), weather(Day,What).
show([ ]) :- nl.
show([Head|Tail]) :- write(Head), tab(1), show(Tail).
```

```
go :- process(Outlook), show(['Outlook:']), write(Outlook).
?- go.
What day's weather do you want?
tuesday.
Outlook:
fair
yes
```

Notice that this user interface still requires the user to type tuesday with a lower-case first letter and follow it with a period.

EXERCISES 8.3

1. Write a program that asks the user what month his or her birthday is and responds either "That's this month." or "That's a while yet." whichever is appropriate.
2. Rewrite rules as necessary to make "fair" appear on the same line as "Outlook:" in the example in this section.

8.4 CHARACTER INPUT AND OUTPUT

The most flexible way to handle input and output is one character at a time. A *character* in programming is a letter (upper or lower case), a numeral, one of the set of special symbols like punctuation, or one of a set of non-printing characters. These non-printing characters have meaning in a computer system, typically representing some control function. For example, "return" has a non-printing character and so does "back-space."

The internal representation for characters in the computer is as integers. Each character has a unique integer associated with it. A standard has been set up, called the *American Standard Code for Information Interchange,* so that different computers use the same representation. There is a chart showing the ASCII (pronounced ask-key) code in Appendix A of this book.

In Prolog, we can have constants that are strings. A *string* is a sequence of characters, handled as a unit. It is written with double quotes around it and can contain any of the printing characters. For example

```
song_line(first, "Row,Row,Row your boat").
```

The internal representation of this string is as a list of integers. That means that if we ask

```
?- song_line(first,What).
What=[82,111,119,44,82,111,119,44,82,111,119,32,121,
       111,117,114,32,98,111,95,116]
```

This is not improving our user interface. We need to have the ASCII codes translated back to characters for printing. There is a built-in predicate that does this translation, **put**. **Put** takes a single integer and writes the associated character to the output stream.

```
?- put(65).
A
```

Since the string is stored as a list of these integer ASCII codes, we can combine our typical list manipulation methods with the predicate, **put**, to print a string.

```
print_string([ ]).
print_string([Head|Tail]) :- put(Head),
    print_string(Tail).
?- print_string("Row,Row").
Row,Row
```

Accepting input character-by-character requires use of built-in predicates, **get**, which gets the next incoming printing character and **get0**, which gets the next incoming character, printing or not. Note that this is get-zero, not get-oh. These predicates each take a single integer, the ASCII code, as arguments. Like **read**, they can also be used to check for a match with the incoming value if the argument is instantiated when the goal is activated.

Using these predicates, we can accept a user response character-by-character until the next character indicates that the user has finished the response. In the program below, the line end is recognized as an ASCII 31. In the version of Prolog where this program was run, "return" is interpreted as "unit separator". Other Prolog versions interpret "return" in other ways. To find out the ASCII code for the line end on your system, query **get0(X)** and respond to the input prompt with a return. The ASCII code will be reported as X

This program appends characters to the list one-by-one.

```
response([First|Rest]) :- get(First),
    get0(Second),
    remain(Second,Rest).
remain(Ch,Word) :- line-end(Ch,Word), !.
remain(Ch,[Ch|Word]) :- get0(Next),
    remain(Next,Word).
line_end(31,[ ]).
```

This program is different conceptually from the ones we saw in Section 8.2 (that used **repeat**) because it is based on recursion. Remain is defined in terms of remain. One could picture the processing of copy, the procedure in Section 8.2 as a zig-zag path moving over and over from **repeat** to handle and back again Remain, in contrast, moves down along the remainder of the sequence, then moves back up to the beginning. One picture of remain's processing is the telescope image we discussed in Chapter 5. Notice also that response must be able to get at least one character, called first, if any processing is going to be done.

This program still does not handle many possible characters or problems that can appear in getting input from a user. For example, backspace or erase would not be handled at all.

Get and **get0**, like all of these input/output predicates, can only be satisfied once. When a string of characters is going to be processed, the programmer has to keep control over the values, as each time **get** is activated, the previous character will be lost.

EXERCISES 8.4

1. Write a program that opens a file as the input stream, reads a character string from the file and writes the string to another file.
2. Write a program that checks the first characters of a file and aborts if they are not the letters HAL.

SUMMARY

Input and output represent the communication between a computer system and the person using the system. In Prolog there are two kinds of data to be communicated: the database and the question/answer interaction. Communication of the database is done primarily by consulting files, including the user as a file. Communication of question/answers is controlled by associating the input and output streams to files or to the user.

There are built-in predicates for modifying the database and for specific writing to and reading from the input and output streams. Some of these predicates handle data character-by-character and others are designed for larger Prolog units. Input and output are concerns in the programming environment and user interface.

EXERCISES CHAPTER 8

1. Each of the following terms is followed by a number of statements. Find ALL of the statements that are true about the terms.
   a) character
      1) represented in ASCII
      2) must be enclosed in single quotes
      3) may need to be enclosed in single quotes
      4) could be non-printing

    b) input stream
      1) may be a file
      2) may be a user
      3) may be source of questions
      4) may be accessed character by character
    c) user interface
      1) requires everything be in same form
      2) requires use of files
      3) requires use of characters
      4) facilitates communication between user and Prolog

2. Complete the chart below.

	Terms	Strings
external representation	hello Jean	hello Jean
internal representation		
written in program		
predicate for input		
predicate for output		

3. Following the three steps below, write a program to build a database of facts of the form

        `made_of(<fruit>,<products>).`

    a) Write a user interface requesting the pairs of fruit and product.
    b) Take the pairs the user enters and build facts in the database from them.
    c) When the user indicates the facts are all complete, write the facts out to a file.

Doing Arithmetic

The purpose of this chapter is to help the learner:
- understand the mechanism by which Prolog can be used for
  number manipulation
  number calculation and
  expression evaluation.
- recognize the operators built into the Prolog system.
- understand operator precedence, position and associativity.

9.1 INTEGER ARITHMETIC

Number manipulation and calculations can be done within all Prolog systems. While some versions of Prolog do more complex arithmetic, all versions can do *integer arithmetic*. That means all numbers are whole numbers. There are no fractions or decimal points. The range from smallest to largest integer useable in a Prolog program depends on the particular Prolog system, but a wide enough range is available to use for the kinds of things a Prolog programmer wants.

Built-in predicates are provided that do arithmetic operations, such as adding, and number comparisons, such as equal to. Conceptually, the predicates can be fit into the Prolog model of defining a predicate, say for multiplication, then having a list of facts to look for a match. This is the same method we use when we learn a "times-table" and remember facts as we need them. Actually, instead of looking them up in a table, computers are finding these values (counting on their fingers as it were) but the effect is the same: the integer arithmetic database is available to use.

Calculation

To do calculation, a built-in predicate, **is**, is used. For example,

```
Sum is 3 + 4.
```

The predicate, **is**, is an infix operator. An operator is a Prolog predicate that is specially set up so that it can be used without the normal syntax for predicates, which is

```
<predicate>(<arguments>).
```

Among operators, we can use *infix* which means the operator appears between its arguments, *prefix*, where the operator appears before the arguments, or *postfix*, when the operator appears after the arguments.

```
infix     3 + 4
prefix    + 3 4
postfix   3 4 +
```

Infix, prefix, and postfix are the possible *positions* for operators. In doing arithmetic in Prolog, we use infix because that is the form we are most used to using to do arithmetic. However, this is optional and the other forms can be used.

In the example

```
Sum is 3 + 4.
```

there are two infix operators, **is** and **+**. The generic form for the is operator is

```
<variable> is <integer expression>.
```

When the goal containing the **is** is activated, the integer expression must be *evaluable*; that is, it must be possible for Prolog, following evaluation rules, to turn the expression into an integer value. This means the expression cannot contain any uninstatiated variables or non-integer constant values.

The first thing that happens when an **is** predicate is activated is that the integer expression is evaluated. In this example, 3 + 4 is evaluated to 7. Then one of two things happens. If the variable Sum is instantiated, the two values are compared, and if they match, the goal succeeds. Obviously, the variable must be instantiated to an integer for this to be possible. For example, given the rule

```
check(Sum) :- Sum is 3 + 4.
?- check(7).
yes
?- check(3).
no
```

If the variable is not instantiated, **is** instantiates it to the value from the expression.

```
?- check(What).
What = 7
```

The integer expression may, and usually does, contain variables along with integers and operators. All variables in the expression, however, must have integer values before the **is** predicate is activated.

Integer Expressions
The generic form for an integer expression is

```
<integer expression><infix operator><integer expression>.
```

The standard selection for infix integer operators is:

+	addition
−	subtraction
*	multiplication
/	division for quotient
mod	division for remainder

Addition, subtraction and multiplication are easy but the two division operators may deserve explanation. Integer arithmetic involves only whole numbers and division rarely "comes out even."

67/5 evaluates to 13	(the integer quotient from division)
67 mod 5 evaluates to 2	(the remainder from division)
15 mod 5 evaluates to 0	(the remainder from division)

To return to the generic form

`<integer expression><infix operator><integer expression>.`

we see that the arguments of the operator can be expressions themselves. For example,

2+3 * 4+6

This is ambiguous, however, as we cannot tell how the "sub-expressions" are meant to be grouped.

(2) + (3*4+6) or
(2+3) * (4+6) or
(2+3*4) + (6)

There are two ways the ambiguity can be resolved. The first is to add in the parentheses that will group the expressions correctly. The second is to know and use the patterns written into the Prolog interpreter.

The patterns have standards in two areas, precedence and associativity. *Precedence* tells, given more than one kind of operator, which will be done first. Among these operators, **mod** has highest precedence, multiplication and division for quotient, which have the same precedence are next, then add and subtract, which also have precedence equal to each other, are lowest. Complex expressions are evaluated according to these precedence rules.

Precedence table

MOD

* /

+ −

---

3 + 2 * 6	**13 mod 3 − 1**
3 + 12	**1 − 1**
15	**0**

Associativity tells, given more than one operator of the same precedence, which will be done first. The precedence might be the same because the operators are in the same precedence class or because they are the same operator. All these operators are left associative, so under associativity, these operators will be done in the order they appear left to right.

```
6 * 6/2                          4 + 3 - 1
36/2                             7 - 1
18                               6

17 mod 3 mod 2                   4/2/2
2 mod 2                          2/2
0                                1
```

As a programming practice, it is better to use parentheses to group expressions, even if they are not necessary to force correct evaluation, because they help people understand the expression better and thus promote fewer errors.

The following example uses a database from which to do calculations.

```
dimension (living_room,15,18,12).
dimension(kitchen,8,8,8).
dimension(bed_room,10,12,8).
floor(Room,Area) :- dimension(Room,Wid,Len,Hig),
     Area is Wid*Len.
wall(Room,Area) :- dimension(Room,Wid,Len,Hig),
     Area is (2*(Wid*Hig))+(2*(Len*Hig)).
?- floor(kitchen,Area).
Area = 64
?- wall(living_room,Space).
Space = 792
```

EXERCISES 9.1

1. What will be the values for these expressions?
   ```
   (2) + (3 * 4 + 6)
   (2 + 3) * 4 + 6
   (2 + 3 * 4) + 6 mod 2
   ```
2. Write a program that shows your answers in Exercise 1 agree with Prolog's evaluation.

9.2 COMPARING INTEGER VALUES

A second way of making use of integers in Prolog is to compare values. One integer value can be compared against another value, testing equal, greater or less than. The operators for these tests are built-in in Prolog.

=:=	equals
=\=	does not equal
>	is greater than
<	is less than
>=	is greater than or equal
=<	is less than or equal

Note the operators that are made of two characters; the order in which the characters appear is important. They cannot be reversed.

These operators that do comparison can be used only on specific integer values. Thus, to compare an expression, it is necessary to use **is** to force the evaluation before a comparison can be done. Each expression being compared must have a value at the time of the comparison, not be an expression.

```
acheck :- (7) = (3+4)
bcheck :- Y is (3+4), Y=7
?- acheck
        no
?- bcheck
        yes
```

In this example, acheck failed because (3 + 4) is an expression and was not evaluated to a value as it was in bcheck.

Comparing directly against an integer from a fact in the database provides direct comparisons. Variables can be instatiated to integers, as in this example which rates people according to their scores.

```
rating(Person,'ACE') :- score(Person,Points), Points>1000.
rating(Person,'NOVICE') :- score(Person,Points), Points<100.
rating(Person,'OK') :- score(Person,Points),
      Points =< 1000, Points >= 100.
score(char,1100).
  .
  .
  .
?- rating(char,Rate).
Rate = ACE
yes
?- rating(Who,'ACE').
Who = char
yes
```

Extracting Number Values

One appropriate use of arithmetic in Prolog is for the analysis of a collection of facts in a database. Say we had a database with many facts of this form.

```
score(<person>,<points>).
```

We might, for example, want to find the average score for all people in the database. The attack this program takes is to gather all the scores into a bag, then find the average from there.

```
score(char,1100).
   :
average(Val) :- bagof(N,S^(score(S,N)),B),
      length(B,C),
      sum(B,T),
      Val is T/C.
length([ ],0).
length([H|T],S) :- length(T,R), S is R + 1.
sum([ ],0).
sum([H|T],S) :- sum(T,R), S is R + H.
```

This program definition says that we can find the average score by gathering a list of the scores, getting the number of scores from the length of the list, summing up all the values in the list and then dividing the sum by the number. For applying **is**, we must be sure the total and the count have values so the average can be found. The last four lines of the database are the rules for finding these values.

EXERCISES 9.2

1. Design facts and rules to calculate the average high temperature for a week.
2. Given a base of facts of the form
   ```
   person(<name>,<age>).
   ```
   write a rule to find out if one person is twice as old as another.
3. Using the database from Exercise 2, write a rule that would report everyone who is more than ten years older than a particular person?

9.3 USING ARITHMETIC IN DATA MANIPULATION

Many of the tasks for which computers are used focus on the processing of numbers. While other computer languages are much better for "number crunching," a programmer using Prolog may want to do some of these same tasks. One such task is sorting a set of number values into ascending order. In Chapter 7, we noted that some Prolog systems have a sort predicate built-in. Here, as an example, is another sort.

This sort is called an insertion sort. It works by going to the tail of a list, then moving backward toward the head of the list, taking each element in turn and putting it into the tail in the place it belongs.

```
ins_sort([ ],[ ]).
ins_sort([Head|Tail],New_list) :-
        ins_sort(Tail,New_tail),
        insert(Head,New_tail,New_list).
```

```
insert(Elem,[Val|List1],[Val|List2] :-
        Elem >= Val, !,
        insert(Elem,List1,List2).
insert(Elem,List,[Elem|List]).
?- ins_sort([3,9,6],Result).
Result = [3,6,9]
yes
```

The predicate, insert, works by moving down the list to find the place for the new element. It moves as long as the element is greater than the head of the list. Since this list is sorted already, as soon as the comparison fails, all the rest of the list belongs beyond the element to be inserted, so the second part of the insert definition puts it into the list there.

EXERCISES 9.3

1. How could ins_sort be modified to sort numbers into decreasing instead of increasing order?
2. How would ins_sort's behavior be different if > = were replaced by > ?
3. What would be required to make ins_sort sort elements within character strings?
4. What would be required to make ins_sort sort constant names?

9.4 AN ARITHMETIC EXAMPLE

Suppose we have a Prolog database that contains information about the presidents of the United States in the form:

```
president(<name>,<birth year>,
          <year began office>,<year left office>).
```

From this base, we can derive several kinds of information.

How long was a president in office:

```
length_office(Name,Years) :- president(Name,_,In,Out),
        Years is Out-In.
```

How old was a particular president when he took office:

```
age(Name,Years) :- president(Name,Birth,In,_),
        Years is In-Birth.
```

Which president was a certain age when he took office:

same rule, switch variables in the question.
use age(Who,65) instead of age(johnson,What).

Which president wa.. younger than fifty when he took office.

```
young(Name) :- president(Name,Birth,In,_),
        Years is In-Birth, Years=<50.
```

Which president served a part term:

```
fractional(Name) :- president(Name,_,In,Out),
        Part is (Out-In) mod 4, Part =\= 0.
```

Who was president in a certain year:

```
in_office(Name,Year) :- president(Name,_,In,Out),
        Year =< Out, Year >= In.
```

This is the first of the two-argument rules here that cannot be used in the reverse direction.

```
?- in_office(kennedy,1962).
?- in_office(Who,1955).
Who = eisenhower
yes
?- in_office(kennedy,When).
** Error: evaluate(_31)
no
```

This error occurred because the variable, When, was instatiated to Year instead of a value. When a comparison was made, the lack of a value caused an error. Such errors as these are easy to make when doing arithmetic. The programmer must be alert to the bias that integer evaluation has as part of its structure.

SUMMARY
Prolog provides facility to do integer arithmetic, using predefined operators for doing calculations and comparing integer values. Integer expressions are evaluated when the is predicate is activated; otherwise, they are Prolog structures like any other.

EXERCISES CHAPTER 9 ▰▰▰▰▰▰▰▰▰▰

1. What will be Prolog's response to these questions?
```
?- V is (3 + 4) mod 2.
?- V is (3 + 4) / 2.
?- V is 3, V < 3.
?- V is 3, V =< 3.
?- V =:= 5.
?- V is 5, V =:= 5.
```

2. Write Prolog programs for these five problems.

   a) Given an integer greater than zero, use a formula to find the sum of all the integers starting with 1 and ending with the integer givén. If the integer is called N, the formula to find this sum is

$$\frac{N * (N + 1)}{2}$$

   b) Write another solution to the same problem, this time recursively adding the numbers up to N. That is, the sum for N is the same as the sum for N − 1 with N added to it.

   c) Make up a database of costs of items in a store, such as a clothing store. Write rules to find the total cost for several items and one to calculate a specific discount, say 20% off.

   d) The factorial of a number is defined to be the product of all the integers starting with 1, continuing up to the number. Recursively, the factorial of a number (say 5) is found by multiplying the number times the factorial of the next lower integer (here 4; 4 factorial is 24, 5 factorial is 120). Write a recursive rule for factorial, using the stopping case of 1 factorial being 1.

   e) Modify your factorial rule to protect it against receiving an argument less than 1.

Building Larger Programs

The purpose of this chapter is to help the learner:
- understand how programs can be developed in modules.
- learn to use problem solving tactics.
- be familiar with debugging tactics, general and Prolog specific.
- consider programming style issues such as
  name choices and physical layout.
  documentation.
  ease of use and robustness.

10.1 DESIGNING PROGRAMS

As programs get larger they contain more and different ideas that the programmer has to put together. Parts of programs are related to or dependent on other parts, and with a large number of parts, interconnectedness results in increased complexity. If one particular part, say a multiple-definition predicate, is subtle in the way it works, any confusion it causes to people reading it may carry over to confusion about the rest of the program.

These factors, length, interconnectedness, and subtlety all add to the *cognitive complexity* of a program. Programs that are large and handle significant problems are bound to be more complex than short ones that do trivial problems.

Complexity, however, makes programs harder to write, more apt to have errors, and harder to discover any errors in. It also makes it harder for a person to read and understand a program. The person reading the program might be an individual who is not the one who wrote the program or it might be the programmer, who, after some length of time, goes back to reuse the program.

To reduce these problems, programmers can follow some established software development practices. These practices, which are also used by programmers who write in other programming languages, fall into two general categories: structure and style.

Modularity

The main goal in good program structure is modularity. *Modularity* means that a program is made up of units separated according to the function they handle. Prolog has some modularity inherent in its structure. A Prolog sentence has the function of defining the term that is the head of the sentence. For example,

```
mono_feet(Hue) :- color(Footgear,Hue).
    shade(sox,Hue).
```

One Prolog sentence cannot define more than one term, as only one term can be in the head of the sentence.

Frequently, of course, we need a multiple rule definition for a term.

```
append([ ],L,L).
append([H|L1],L2,[H|L3]) :- append(L1,L2,L3).
```

These two sentences between them define append.

Similarly, a group of facts with the same predicate defines the meaning of that predicate by declaring all the cases where it is true.

```
weather(monday,fair).
weather(tuesday,cloudy).
:
```

These three examples, the simple rule, the multiple rule and the group of facts, show the fundamental units from which Prolog programs are built.

Looking at rules, we recognize that the terms in the body of the rules sometimes include terms that are references to other definitions. For example the
mono__feet rule makes reference to color and shade as part of its definition.
For the mono__feet rule to be functional, the definitions of color and shade
must also be available.

From these examples, we can see that a module in Prolog is easy to delineate.
The module for a function includes the rule(s) that defines it and the definitions of any terms that appear in the body of the rule.

Larger modules are built of smaller modules. In Chapter 5, for example, we
saw a module

```
palindrome(Half,Whole) :- reverse(Half,Rest),
    append(Half,Rest,Whole).
```

The palindrome module is made up of this rule, the reverse module and the
append module. Modules form a hierarchy in which higher units are lower
units aggregated together.

The modularity available in Prolog is not, however, all that it might be. The
problem is that, even though we as programmers understand the hierarchy
that has low-level modules as part of higher-level modules, we have no way
to communicate this to Prolog. We might, for example, have a module that
checks spelling which includes

```
test(<word>,suffix) :- .....
```

At the same time, we might have a separate module to keep track of self-study
progress that includes

```
test(<subject>,completed) :- .......
```

We know which "test" belongs with which module but Prolog does not. It has
access to any predicate in the program at any time and will always take the
first match it comes to.

A programmer who is careful and working on small problems can readily control this problem, but it will frequently appear in complex problems or programs where more than one programmer is contributing.

Specifying that low-level modules belong inside higher-level modules and
should not be used by other modules is called *encapsulation*. Even though
Prolog modules cannot be encapsulated, the basic process of building programs
in modules is an effective way of developing a Prolog program.

Bottom Up and Top Down

Continuing this process of building modules on modules, we see that a program, however large, is built of smaller modules. Creating a program by building modules, then integrating them in larger modules, is called *bottom-up* programming.

Rarely, however, do we use this method by itself to write a program. Bottom-up programming lends itself to exploration and serendipity, while most programming is focused on a specific objective. When we write a significant program, our task is to solve a problem that is expressed at the top of the hierarchy. To get from this starting point down to the fundamental units that the structure is built on, we use a process called *top-down design*. The purpose of top-down design is to give the programmer a clear understanding of the program, its component parts and the way those components fit together.

In working top-down, a critical part of the strategy is to be willing to put off consideration of specific details when larger units are being considered. One tactic that is often helpful in supporting focus on units rather than detail is to draw a diagram.

Say we were working on a program that accepted a question and returned an answer, with the question and answer in English sentences. At the top level we could diagram this program as in Figure 10.1.

Figure 10.1

Top Level of Problem

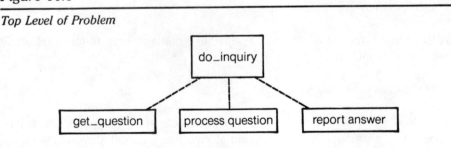

At this level, we need not concern ourselves with details of the modules in the bottom level of the diagram. We do need to be sure the modules below add up to the one above and we should be concerned about communication between the modules. We might improve the diagram by writing in the arguments for each definition along the communication lines.

Figure 10.2

Top Level with Information Passing

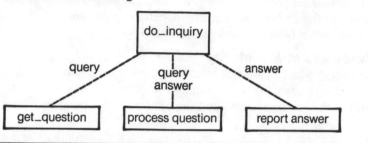

From this diagram, we can write the rule for the module that is the whole program.

```
do_inquiry :- get_question(Query),
    process_question(Query,Answer),
    report_answer(Answer).
```

There is more to this module, however, as definitions of the three component modules are needed. These can be designed top-down, too. For example, see Figure 10.3.

Figure 10.3

Get Question Module

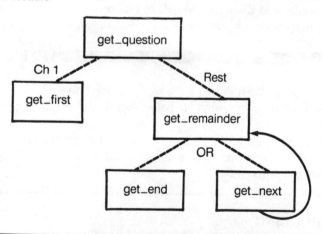

The module for getting a string of characters from the user involves getting the first printing character and then getting characters repeatedly until the character that indicates the end is found. Similar analysis of the other modules to process the question and to repeat the Answer would also be done. There is nothing magic about the particular diagrams shown here. Individual people will have particular kinds of diagrams and notational systems they find helpful. Using some kind of diagram does, however, facilitate the programmer's understanding of the problem by focusing attention on the component modules and the relationship between parts of the modules.

Advantages of Modularity

Top-down design helps the programmer comprehend and develop the modularity in a program. This reductionistic approach to problem solving can benefit both the effectiveness and the efficiency of a programmer's effort.

Most important, it limits the complexity of what the programmer must be able to think about at one time. Ignoring the details of one module while working on another saves cognitive load. In a like manner, the independence of modules allows more than one programmer to work on a program, with individuals building modules to fit together according to the definition given for a higher-level module.

Another advantage of modularity is that modules, once written, can be used again in other programs that include the same component. The module that is specified above, get__question, is like a program developed in Chapter 8. It can be used in this program, sparing the programmer its rewriting.

A final and very useful facet of modules is that they can be written into Prolog and tested independent of other modules. For example, the palindrome program could be written in three steps: the append module written and tested; the reverse module written and tested; the palindrome rule added, creating the top-level module, and the whole tested. In this process we have returned to do bottom-up programming guided by our top-down design.

EXERCISES 10.1

1. Diagram a top-down design for a well-balanced meal.
2. Diagram a top-down design for palindromes with an uneven number of letters.
3. Given a procedure to do even-numbered palindromes and the one from above for uneven-numbered, write a procedure to check strings to see if they are palindromes.

10.2 DEBUGGING

If a programmer does a good top-down design and an accurate translation of the design into Prolog the resulting program will not have errors in it. Errors, which in programming are called *bugs,* do in reality appear.

Bugs can result from errors in the design of the program or from incorrect translation of the design into Prolog. Debugging a program is usually an interesting problem-solving task itself. It requires observing the behavior of the program, inferring relationships between the behavior and parts of the program, hypothesizing a correction and testing the correction. Effective debugging concentrates on the first two of these four steps rather than the last two.

Observing Program Behavior

There are three sources of information about how a program is behaving:

- messages from Prolog
- results of test cases
- traces of program executions

Messages from Prolog are most apparent. A typical message

```
syntax error
```

indicates Prolog found some character in the program that did not fit the Prolog syntax rules. Similarly, messages about running out of space or not being able to read from a specified file provide the programmer with information that may point toward the bug. Error messages from Prolog are sometimes distractors, however, because the actual error might occur earlier than where Prolog recognized a problem. For example, the first time the programmer keyed in the module from Chapter 9 that does insertion sort, it looked like this

```
ins_sort([ ],[ ]).
ins_sort([Head|Tail],[New_list]) :-
      ins_sort(Tail,New_tail),
      insert(Head,New_tail,New_list).
insert(Elem,[Val|List1],[Val|List2]) :-
      Elem >= Val, !,
      insert(Elem,List1,List2).
insert(Elem,L,[Elem|L]).
```

The program was loaded from a file and no problems were evident (nor expected). The interaction testing the program looked like this

```
?- ins_sort([3,6,5],L).
**Error: evaluate ([6,[5]]).
no
?- listing(insert).
insert(_1,[_2|_3],[_2|_4]) :-
      _1 >= _2, !,
      insert(_1,_3,_4).
insert(_1,_2,[_1|_2]).
yes
?- insert(4,[2,6],X).
X = [2,4,6]
yes
```

```
?- insert(8,[ ],X).
X = [8]
yes
?- listing(ins_sort).
ins_sort([ ],[ ]).
ins_sort([_1|_2],[_3]) :-
ins_sort(_2,_4),
insert(_1,_4,_3).
```

The error message indicated that the problem was in trying to evaluate an arithmetic expression which is in the insert module. The listing of that module did not show an obvious error, so the programmer gave the insert module a test case. The module handled that case correctly, as it did the next test case, convincing the programmer the problem must be elsewhere. The definition of ins_sort was the only other choice here, and from a careful look at the definition the problem, a spare set of square brackets, [_3], was discovered in the term.

After the fact, it is easy to see that the original message fit the error. Like many a puzzle, the answer is obvious once you know the answer.

Trying various test cases is a powerful way of pinning down a bug. When a module contains a multiple rule, only part of the cases may use the rule with the problem, so varying test cases may focus attention on the buggy definition. Trying test cases and observing results allows elimination of areas where the bug is not. This is an example of a standard problem-solving technique, using inference to limit the search space.

Another standard debugging tactic is to trace the process of the program execution. Execution in this usage means to carry out or perform. To trace a program, one must be viewing it procedurally and considering steps between a question and a response.

Programs can be traced by hand, with the programmer simulating the machine under control of the Prolog program. The programmer follows the flow of control, noting instantiations and backtracking as appropriate. The problem with hand simulations is that the programmer is apt to do what he or she knows the program should do rather than what it in fact would do.

Many programming environments provide facility for the reporting to the programmer of the actual flow of control and instantiations during a program execution. This is usually very helpful because the programmer knows how the trace should look and any divergence is immediately apparent.

Here is an example of a trace using part of an earlier example doing arithmetic over a database about presidents.

```
president(eisenhower,1890,1953,1961).
president(kennedy,1917,1961,1963).
president(johnson_lb,1908,1963,1969).
in_office(Name,Year) :- president(Name,_,In,Out),
           Year =< Out, Year >= In.
| ?- trace.
yes
| ?- in_office(Who,1962).
   (1) 0 Call : in_office(_24,1962) ?
   (2) 1 Call : president(_24,_90,_91,_92) ?
   (2) 1 Exit : president(eisenhower,1890,1953,1961)
   (3) 1 Call : 1962=<1961 ?
   (3) 1 Fail : 1962=<1961
   (2) 1 Redo : president(eisenhower,1890,1953,1961) ?
   (2) 1 Exit : president(kennedy,1917,1961,1963)
   (4) 1 Call : 1962=<1963 ?
   (4) 1 Exit : 1962=<1963
   (5) 1 Call : 1962>=1961 ?
   (5) 1 Exit : 1962>=1961
   (1) 0 Exit : in_office(kennedy,1962)
Who = kennedy
yes
```

This is a full trace, showing all the goals that were activated and resulting
successes and failures. The problem with a machine trace is usually too much
information. Sophisticated tracers or debuggers let the programmer limit the
information that will be provided by specifying segments or components to
report on. To do this, of course, the programmer must have at least some idea
where the problem might be. This is another reason for building and testing a
program in modules.

Tracing is not only useful in debugging; it is also a good learning tool. Watch-
ing a trace of Prolog processing can be edifying especially if the control pattern
is complex. As an auxiliary to a trace, drawing diagrams is frequently helpful.
For example, here is a diagram of the execution of the rule to get a string
from the user.

Figure 10.4

Execution of Get__string

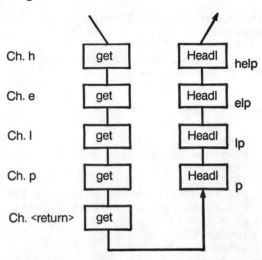

A last and very important debugging tactic is to take a break from looking for the bug. In deducing the relationships between program parts and program behavior, premature conclusions often interfere with the problem solving. Taking a break can allow a new start. Explaining to another person what the program is supposed to be doing is another way of discovering a program bug, especially a logic error. The person hearing the explanation does not need to understand the program; it is in the explaining that the programmer discovers where the bug arose.

Debugging Database Modifiers

When a program uses procedures that modify the contents of the database (e.g. **assert**), all the planning and modular testing can go awry. The modules that have been built and tested may no longer be trustworthy if modifications of the database are made. To try to control entry of bugs in programs that use these "meta-logical" predicates they should be kept as non-pervasive as possible and their use should be carefully documented.

EXERCISES 10.2

1. Hand trace the execution of this program.
```
reverse([ ],[ ]).
reverse([Head|Tail],List) :- reverse(Tail,Result),
        append(Result,[Head],List).
append([ ],List,List).
append([Element|List1],List2,[Element|List3]) :-
        append(List1,List2,List3).
?- reverse([a,b],L).
```

2. Say you had this rule

```
palindrome(List1,List2) :-
            append(List1,List3,List2),
            reverse(List1,List3).
```

and got this result

```
?- palindrome([a,b],Result).
Result = [a,b,a,b,b]
```

what would be some test cases that might help discover the bug.

10.3 DOCUMENTATION

The previous discussion in this chapter has to do with the structure of larger programs. Documentation is one of the facets of programming *style* that is important in writing larger programs. Documentation is a commentary about the program. Programs usually have internal documentation and external documentation.

Internal documentation consists of comments that are written in the Prolog program to give a human reader information about the program. Particular procedures such as predicates that modify the database or uses of cut that eliminate certain options should be noted. Modules should be labeled according to their function.

Because we cannot simply add comments into a program as if they were Prolog sentences, there are special marks to enclose these comments, the /*...*/ brackets.

```
/*This comment will be ignored by Prolog*/
```

The Prolog system simply skips over any characters between the marks. Note that this introduces a new source of bugs: commenting out definitions by mistake.

External documentation usually contains a description of what the program is for, how to use it, and any special characteristics a programmer might need to know about it. It may be in the form of books and manuals, in the form of document files on a system or in the form of introductory information as part of the program, explaining its use. External documentation is important to the long-term value of a program. If a program is going to be used as part of another program or revised with modification, documentation provides the vehicle for knowing how.

Name Choices

The amount of internal documentation needed to make clear the purpose o. program components depends on how the names for constants and variables are chosen. Well-chosen names can communicate a good deal of information to a human using or reading a program. From Prolog's point of view, these two definitions are equivalent.

```
a(X,Y) :- b(X,M),c(Y,M).
uncle(Man,Child) :- brother(Man,Person),
                    parent(Child,Person).
```

The human readers who gain from the communication inherent in well-chose. names include the original programmer.

Physical Layout

A third characteristic of programming style is the physical layout of the Prolog sentences. The two most important rules-of-thumb in program layout are to be consistent and to use empty space generously. Modules should be written as units with blank lines between modules. If a module is quite large, then its component modules should be set off with blank lines themselves. "Quite large" is a very subjective term; twenty facts of the same form is not as large a unit as twenty complex rules.

The physical layout of rules will depend on the complexity of the requirements and the length of the terms. Since rules rarely fit entirely on one line, some decision must be made about where the requirements will be listed. Continuation to the next line, with or without indentation, is one possibility. Another is listing only one term per line, so the requirements form a column on the page.

In general, if a rule has more than five or six requirements in its body, there should probably be another intermediate level of modules in between the rule and the requirements.

Well-written Programs

In addition to having good structure and style, well-written programs are easy to use. Being easy to use includes providing instruction at the level needed by the user, and being robust enough so that a small error by the user does not result in disaster.

Structure, style and other design decisions depend on the individual who is programming the problem solution. Different people prefer different structure and style patterns. Programmers will also be forced to make tradeoffs on desirable program characteristics. For example, speed of response may be lost as more humane user interfaces are built. Nonetheless, the programmer must be aware of these concerns.

EXERCISES 10.3

1. Rewrite this program with good physical arrangement and documentation.
   ```
   rev([ ],[ ]).
   app([ ],X,X).
   palin(X,X2) :- app(X,L3,X2), rev(X,L3).
   rev([H|T],L) :- rev(T,Out), app(Out,[H],L)
   app([E|X],X2,[E|L3]) :- app(X,X2,L3).
   ```
2. Break this rule up into three modules and write a rule to call the modules.
   ```
   have_groceries :- cereal(Brand),
                     juice(Fruit),
                     caffeine(Drink),
                     sandwich(Filling),
                     milk(white),
                     supper_dish(Pasta),
                     pie(Type).
   ```
3. Add one more requirement to have_groceries, that Fruit is not instantiated to the same constant as Type, and rewrite the have_groceries rule you wrote in Exercise 2 to handle this.

10.4 AN EXAMPLE OF PROGRAM DEVELOPMENT

A typical programming project starts out with an ill-defined problem. The problem must be explored and clarified before the top-down analysis can be done.

Problem:

We want an editor that replaces jargon with non-technical words.

Clarification: is there a one-to-one replacement list for the jargon and non-technical equivalents? Yes.

Clarification: what units will be handled? Sentences.

Clarification: where will the sentences come from? The user.

Clarification: where will the edited sentences be reported? The user.

Clarification: should the user interface include prompts or a comment along with the answer? Just "Type in a sentence." and "The edited sentence is:".

Clarification: how is the sentence delineated? Ends with a period.

Clarification: will the sentence be more than one line long? No.

Clarification: should I worry about commas and other special symbols? Not this time.

Preliminary breakdown of the problem·
  get the string
  make changes
  display the changed string

Decision: internal representation for the changing module will have words as items in a list.

Decision: the input module will be responsible for changing the character input to atoms. For symmetry, the display module will take care of format from the atomic form.

Analysis of the middle module:

Go down the list, switching words to be edited out for their replacements. Work recursively to the end. Any word without a replacement just gets copied.

Decide to build this part and test it.

Recursive rule needs stopping case.

```
edit([ ],[ ]).
edit([Old|Tail],[New|New_tail]) :-
      swap(Old,New),
      edit(Tail,New_tail).
```

A set of facts of the form swap(<old>,<new>) will specify each of the jargon words and its replacement.

To handle words not changed.

1. put non-change rule at bottom of list so any change rules encountered first
2. should return same value if no changes
    swap(Any,Any).

Write the module, provide a few words to swap and test.

```
edit([ ],[ ]).
edit([Old|Tail],[New|New_tail]) :-
        swap(Old,New), edit(Tail,New_tail).
swap(groovy,exciting).
swap(ugly,unattractive).
swap(Any,Any).
?- edit([this,is,groovy],Result).
Result = [this,is,exciting]
```

Analysis of input module:

The input module includes prompting the user, getting the input and transforming it into a list of atoms. The first part is already done, from Chapter 8, so it can be reused with a little modification.

```
string_print([ ]).
string_print([H|T]):-put(H),string_print(T).
inquire(List) :- prompt, sentence(List).
prompt :- string_print("Please type a sentence."),nl.
```

The second part gets character strings in word units, then transfers them to atoms using the predicate, **name**. This routine was developed in Chapter 8.

```
sentence(Units) :- get(Ch), lc(Ch,Ch_lc), words(Ch_lc,Units).
words(31,[ ]).          /* end of entry */
words(C,[P|Rest]) :- one_word(C,L),
      name(P,L), get0(C_next), words(C_next,Rest).
one_word(32,[ ]).       /* space character */
one_word(46,[ ]).       /* period */
one_word(C,[C|Rest]) :- get0(C2), one_word(C2,Rest).
lc(Cap,Little) :- Cap>64, Cap<91, Little is Cap+32.
                        /* ASCII lower case is upper case + 32 */
lc(Little,Little).
?-sentence(What).
|: This is it.
What = [this,is,it]
yes
```

Analysis of output module:

The output comment is done in the same manner as the prompt in the input module. The first atom is capitalized to make the sentence start, then each atom in the list is output, with a following period. Alternatives for format of the output can be considered.

```
show(Result) :- comment, respond(Result).
comment :- nl, string_print("The edited sentence is:"), nl.
respond([First|Rest]) :- first_word(First), output(Rest).
first_word(Unit) :- capitalize(Unit,UC_unit),
                    tab(5), write(UC_unit).
output([ ]) :- write('.'), !.
output([One|Rest]) :- write(' '),write(One), output(Rest).
capitalize(LC_word,UC_word) :- name(LC_word,[Start|Rest]),
                    Letter is Start - 32,
                    name(UC_word,[Letter|Rest])
?- show([this,one]).
    This one.
yes
```

Specification of the top-level module:

Finally, the main rule is written, combining the modules already designed and tested.

```
go :- inquire(Sentence), edit(Sentence,Result), show(Result).
```

The final program, ready to have the dictionary specified with the needed vocabulary:

```
/* edit module and dictionary */
swap(groovy,exciting).
swap(ugly,unattractive).
swap(Any,Any).
edit([ ],[ ]).
edit([Old|Tail],[New|New_tail]) :-
  swap(Old,New), edit(Tail,New_tail).

/*string print utility*/
string_print([ ]).
string_print([H|T]):-put(H),string_print(T).

/* input module */
inquire(List) :- prompt, sentence(List).
prompt :- string_print("Please enter a sentence.").nl.
sentence(Units) :- get(Ch), lc(Ch,Ch_lc), words(Ch_lc,Units).
words(31,[ ]).            /* end of entry */
words(C,[P|Rest]) :- one_word(C,L),
    name(P,L), get0(C_next), words(C_next,Rest).
one_word(32,[ ]).        /* space character */
one_word(46,[ ]).        /* period */
one_word(C,[C|Rest]) :- get0(C2), one_word(C2,Rest).
lc(Cap,Little) :- Cap>64, Cap<91, Little is Cap+32.
                    /* ASCII lower case is upper case + 32 */
lc(Little,Little).

/* output module */
show(Result) :- comment, respond(Result).
comment :- nl, string_print("The edited sentence is:"), nl.
respond([First|Rest]) :- first_word(First), output(Rest).
first_word(Unit) :- capitalize(Unit,UC_unit), tab(5),
            write(UC_unit).
output([ ]) :- write('.'), !.
output([One|Rest]) :- write(' '),write(One), output(Rest).
capitalize(LC_word,UC_word) :- name(LC_word,[Start|Rest]),
                    Letter is Start - 32,
                    name(UC_word,[Letter|Rest]).

/* main definition */
go :- inquire(Sentence), edit(Sentence,Result), show(Result).
```

SUMMARY

Large programs are built out of modules which in Prolog are smaller programs themselves. Careful analysis of the problem that we want the program to solve leads to a well structured program.

Program style has the fundamental goal of clearly communicating the program's function to people who will be reading or using the program. A program should be as easy to use as is possible within the other constraints under which the program developer must work.

EXERCISES CHAPTER 10 ▅▅▅▅▅▅▅▅▅▅▅▅▅▅▅▅▅▅▅▅▅▅▅▅▅

1. Write programs for these problems.
    a) A concordance is a listing of words that occur in a text along with a count of the frequency of each word. The words are listed in alphabetical order. Write a program to produce a concordance from a list of words presented as Prolog strings.
    b) Write a program to play tic-tac-toe. For a simple version, have Prolog play second and a only play defensive game.
    c) Write a program that understands simple sentences of the forms:

    _____ is a _____.
    A _____ is a _____.
    Is _____ a _____?

    The program should respond to the questions according to the previously given sentences.
    d) A queen on a chessboard threatens to capture any other piece on the same row, same column or same diagonal as itself. Write a program to find all the ways of placing 4 queens on a 4 × 4 chessboard so that no queen threatens another.
    e) Layout a map of 5 cities, then write a program that plans the route between two towns (entered by user) and reports a route and the total mileage. A simple version would find any one route; a more complex one would find the best route.

APPENDIXES

American Standard Code for Information Interchange

0	NUL	Null	43	+		86	V	
1	SOH	Start heading	44	,		87	W	
2	STX	Start text	45	–		88	X	
3	ETX	End text	46	.		89	Y	
4	EOT	End transmission	47	/		90	Z	
5	ENQ	Inquiry	48	0		91	[	
6	ACK	Acknowledgment	49	1		92	\	
7	BEL	Bell	50	2		93	]	
8	BS	Backspace	51	3		94	↑	
9	HT	Horizontal tab	52	4		95	—	
10	LF	Line feed	53	5		96	`	
11	VT	Vertical tab	54	6		97	a	
12	FF	Form feed	55	7		98	b	
13	CR	Carriage return	56	8		99	c	
14	SO	Shift out	57	9		100	d	
15	SI	Shift in	58	:		101	e	
16	DLE	Data link escape	59	;		102	f	
17	DC1	Device control 1	60	<		103	g	
18	DC2	Device control 2	61	=		104	h	
19	DC3	Device control 3	62	>		105	i	
20	DC4	Device control 4	63	?		106	j	
21	NAK	Neg. acknowledge	64	@		107	k	
22	SYN	Synchronous/Idle	65	A		108	l	
23	ETB	End trans. block	66	B		109	m	
24	CAN	Cancel data	67	C		110	n	
25	EM	End of medium	68	D		111	o	
26	SUB	Start special seq.	69	E		112	p	
27	ESC	Escape	70	F		113	q	
28	FS	File separator	71	G		114	r	
29	GS	Group separator	72	H		115	s	
30	RS	Record separator	73	I		116	t	
31	US	Unit separator	74	J		117	u	
32	SP	Space	75	K		118	v	
33	!		76	L		119	w	
34	"		77	M		120	x	
35	#		78	N		121	y	
36	$		79	O		122	z	
37	%		80	P		123	{	
38	&		81	Q		124			
39	'		82	R		125	}	
40	(		83	S		126	~	
41	)		84	T		127	DEL	
42	*		85	U				

APPENDIX B
Further Reading

Apt, K. R. and van Emden, M. H. Contributions to the theory of logic programming. *Journal of ACM* 29, 841–862, 1982.

Backus, J. Can Programming be liberated from the von Neumann style? *Communications of the ACM*, 21, 613–641, 1978.

Clark, K. L. and McCabe, F. G. *Micro-Prolog: Programming in Logic.* Prentice-Hall, Englewood Cliffs, NJ, 1984.

Clark, K. L. and Tarnlund, S. A. (Editors) *Logic Programming* (APIC Studies in Data Processing, Vol. 16). Academic Press, London, 1982.

Clocksin, W. F. and Mellish, C. S. *Programming in Prolog.* (second edition) Springer-Verlag, Berlin, 1984.

Conery, J. S. and Kibler, D. F. Parallel interpretaton of logic programs. *Proc. ACM Conference on Functional Programming Langauges and Computer Architecture.* Portsmouth, NH, 1981.

Ennals, R. *Beginning Micro-Prolog.* Harper and Row, New York, 1984.

Deliyanni, A. and Kowalski, R. A. Logic and semantic networks, *Communications of the ACM* 22, 184–192, 1979.

Feigenbaum, E. and McCorduck, P. *The Fifth Generation.* Signet, New York, 1984.

Harris, M. D. *An Introduction to Natural Laguage Processing.* Reston, Reston, VA, 1985.

Journal of Logic Programming. North Holland, New York, July 1984—ongoing.

Hoare, C. A. R. An axiomatic basis for computer programming. *Communications of the ACM* 12, 576–580, 1969.

Hogger, C. J. Derivation of logic programs. *Journal of the ACM* 28, 372–422, 1981.

Hogger, C. J. *Introduction to Logic Programming* (APIC Studies in Data Processing, Vol. 21). Academic Press, London, 1984.

International Symposium on Logic Programming. Atlantic City, NJ. IEEE Computer Society Press, New York, 1984.

International Symposium on Logic Programming. Boston, IEEE Computer Society Press, New York, 1985.

Kowalski, R. A. *Logic for Problem Solving*. Elsevier-North Holland, New York, 1979.

Kowalski, R. A. Algorithm = logic + control. *Communications of the ACM 22*, 424–436, 1979.

Li, D. *A PROLOG Database System*. John Wiley and Sons, New York, 1984

Lloyd, J. W. *Foundations of Logic Programming*. Springer-Verlag, Berlin, 1984.

Pereira, L. M. (ed). *Logic Programming Newsletter*. Universidade Nova de Lisboa, Portugal, 1981—ongoing.

Rich, E. *Artificial Intelligence*. McGraw-Hill, New York, 1983.

Robinson, J. A. A machine-oriented logic based on the resolution principle. *Journal of ACM 12*, 23–41, 1965.

Robinson, J. A. *Logic: form and function*. Elsevier-North Holland, New York, 1979.

Warren, D. H. D., Pereira, L. M. and Pereira, F. C. N. PROLOG-the language and its implementation compared with LISP. *Proc. of Symposium on Artificial Intelligence and Programming Languages, SIGPLAN Notices*, 12:8, 1977.

Wos, L., Overbeek, R., Lusk, E. and Boyle, J. *Automated Reasoning*. Prentice-Hall, Englewood Cliffs, NJ, 1984.

Comparison of Different Versions of Prolog

A number of people have written interpreters so that Prolog is available on a wide variety of computers. These interpreters fall into two general categories, those in the Standard Prolog family and those in the micro-Prolog family.

Four of the most common versions of Prolog or micro-Prolog are compared in this section, two from each family. They are:

DECsystem-10/20, the basis for this book and included here for cross-reference;

C-Prolog, very similar to Standard, designed for 32-bit machines such as the VAX;

micro-Prolog, written specifically for microcomputers, using a syntax somewhat different from Standard;

SIMPLE, an extension of micro-Prolog, designed to use a more English-like syntax.

The syntax described in the four sections appears in the order that syntax is introduced in the text, chapter by chapter.

Note: DECsystem-10 and VAX are trademarks of Digital Equipment Corporation.

STANDARD DECsystem-10/20 PROLOG

Chapter 2

Facts	predicate(arguments).
example	`likes(sally,swimming).`
	`friendly(sally).`
	`shops(sally,vegetables,market).`
Constants	begin with a lower-case letter
example	`sally`
Variables	begin with an upper-case letter
example	`Sport`
Query	clause with or without variables follows a ?-
example	`?- likes(sally,swimming).`

single answer	respond with a return

example	```?- likes(sally,Sport).```
	```Sport = swimming```
	```yes```

multiple answer	respond with a semi-colon

example	```?- likes(sally,Sport).```
	```Sport = swimming ;```
	```Sport = tennis ;```
	```no```

Conjunctions	use a comma for "and"
example	```?- likes(Who,swimming),``` ``` brought(Who,suit).```
Creating a database	access Prolog, get prompt |?-
from user (to interactively build database)	```consult(user).``` or ```[user].``` CONTROL Z to stop

example	```| ?- [user].```
	```| likes(sally,swimming).```
	```| ^Z```
	```| ?-```

from file (previously built by editor or saved from past session)	```consult('<file-name>').``` or ``` ['<file-name>'].```
example	```['star.2'].``` ```STAR.2 CONSULTED```

Chapter 3

Rule	```<head> :- <body>.```
example	```gets_exercise(Who) :-``` ``` likes(Who,swimming).```
Rules with conjunction	use comma for conjunction

example	```gets_exercise(Who) :-```
	``` likes(Who,swimming),```
	``` brought(Who,suit).```

Interrupt	```^C``` CONTROL C

Chapter 4

Trace	facility to observe processing
example	```?- trace.``` ```?- get_exercise(Who).```

Chapter 5

List	collection of objects specified in order
example	```[bank,store,florist]```
Head, Tail	special notation
example	```[Head|Tail].```
Empty list	```[ ]```

SIMPLE EXTENSION OF MICRO-PROLOG

Chapter 2

Facts	argument predicate argument or predicate(arguments)
example	Sally likes swimming or likes(Sally swimming) Sally female or female(Sally)
Constants	any word
example	Sally
Variables	one of the letters x, y or z, upper or lower case followed (optionally) by an integer
example	X1
Query	is(Sally likes swimming)
single answer	specify one
example	one(x : x likes swimming)
multiple answer	all possibilities given
example	which(x : Sally likes x) swimming tennis no(more) answers
Conjunctions	use the word AND or &
example	which(x : x likes swimming & x likes tennis)
Creating a database	access Prolog and LOAD SIMPLE prompt is &.
from user (to create interactively)	add(<sentence>)
example	&.add((Sally likes swimming))
from file (previously created with editor or saved from past session)	LOAD <file-name>
example	LOAD STAR
Options	accept, edit

Chapter 3

Rule	<simple sentence> if <sentence>
example	X exercises if X likes swimming
Rules with conjunction	use the word AND
example	X exercises if X likes swimming and X brought suit
Interrupt	^C CONTROL C

Chapter 4

Trace	LOAD TRACE KILL TRACE

Chapter 5

List	items in parentheses separated by spaces
example	(2 3 7)
Head, Tail	(t1| t2)
example	(x| y)
Empty list	( )

C-PROLOG

Chapter 2

Facts	predicate(arguments).
example	likes(sally,swimming). friendly(sally). shops(sally,vegetables,market)
Constants	begin with a lower-case letter
example	sally
Variables	begin with an upper-case letter
example	Sport
Query	clause with or without variables follows a ?
example	?- likes(sally,swimming).
single answer	respond with a return
example	?- likes(sally,Sport). Sport = swimming yes
multiple answer	respond with a semi-colon
example	?- likes(sally,Sport). Sport = swimming ; Sport = tennis ; no
Conjunctions	use a comma for "and"
example	?- likes(Who,swimming), brought(Who,suit).
Creating a database	access Prolog, get prompt |?-
from user (to inter- actively build database)	consult(user). or [user]. END_OF_INPUT (^D) to stop
example		likes(sally,swimming). | ^D | ?-
from file (previously built by editor or saved from past session)	consult('<file-name>'). or ['<file-name>'].
example	['star.2']. STAR.2 CONSULTED

Chapter 3

Rule	`<head> :- <body>.`
example	`gets_exercise(Who) :-` `    likes(Who,swimming).`
Rules with conjunction	use comma for conjunction

example	`gets_exercise(Who) :-`
	`    likes(Who,swimming),`
	`    brought(Who,suit).`

Interrupt	`^D` CONTROL D

Chapter 4

Trace	facility to observe processing
example	`?- trace.` `?- get_exercise(Who).`

Chapter 5

List	collection of objects specified in order
example	`[bank,store,florist]`
Head, Tail	special notation
example	`[Head|Tail].`
Empty list	`[ ]`
Notes:	C-Prolog allows real-number arithmetic

MICRO-PROLOG

Chapter 2

Facts	`((predicate argument1 argument2...))`
example	`(likes Sally swimming)` `(female Sally)`
Constants	alpha character followed by letters or digits
example	Sally
Variables	one of the letters x, y or z, upper or lower case followed (optionally) by an integer
example	X1
Query	`? (likes Sally swimming)`
responses	`?` for no return to prompt for yes
show answer	specify to print variable instantiation
example	`((likes x swimming)(PP x))`
Conjunctions	sequence and enclose in parentheses
example	`((likes x swimming)(likes x tennis)(PP x))`

Creating a database	access Prolog prompt is &.
from user (to create interactively)	((<sentence>))
example	&.((likes Sally swimming))

from file (previously
  created with editor or
  saved from past session)
	LOAD <file-name>

example	LOAD STAR

Chapter 3

Rule	((<head>)(<body>))
example	((exercises X)(likes x swimming))
Rules with conjunction	((<head>)(<bodypt1>)(<bodypt2>)...)
example	((exercises X)(likes X swimming) (brought X suit))
Interrupt	^C CONTROL C

Chapter 4

Trace	LOAD TRACE KILL TRACE

Chapter 5

List	items in parentheses separated by spaces
example	(2 3 7)
Head, Tail	(t1| t2)
example	(x| y)
Empty list	( )

Formalizing Terminology

PROLOG COMPONENT SYNTAX

All components of a Prolog program are built from a few basic units. *Syntax* rules specify how these units can be combined to create other components. Prolog programs are made of terms. *Terms* can be *constants*, *variables* or *structures*. Constants and variables are simple entities; structures are collections of other entities that are aggregated into a single entity.

Constants are written as a sequence of characters. The characters are either alphanumeric (letters and numerals), in which case the sequence starts with a lower-case letter; non-alphanumeric printing characters, (like '+') called signs, in which case the constants are usually made entirely of signs; or all numerals, in which case they are treated as integers.

Constants are either *integers* or *atoms*. If a programmer wants to specify an atom that does not follow the syntax rules for naming (i.e. begin with an upper-case letter or include special characters) the sequence can be enclosed in single quote marks ('Hi'). Blank spaces cannot appear in constant names, but an underscore (___) can be used to represent the space.

Variables are written as an alphanumeric sequence beginning with an upper case letter or with an underscore. In listings, Prolog represents variables as an underscore followed by an integer; the underscore alone is the *anonymous variable*, a place-holder in a structure for a variable of no current relevance.

A structure, sometimes called a *compound term*, is made of a *functor* and *components*. The functor is written first and is followed by the components in parentheses. These components are terms: constants, variables or other structures. In Prolog, *predicates* and their *arguments* are expressed as structures. The predicate is a functor that is special because of its context, at the beginning of the structure. Functors that appear as components in a compound structure are treated as objects instead of as predicates, except in the case of certain built-in predicates such as **not** or **call**. The number of components with a functor is called the *arity* of the functor. Functors with two arguments are sometimes written as *operators* in *infix* form. These appear frequently in arithmetic expressions such as A + B.

Lists are an important type of structure in Prolog. They are made up of *elements* which are Prolog terms (i.e. constants, variables or structures). A list is either the empty list, noted as **[ ]**, or is a structure with a *head* and *tail*. The head and tail are the arguments of the functor named **.**, the dot. Using the dot notation, a list of the elements X, Y, Z is written

> (X, . (Y, . (Z, [ ]))) .

By definition, the empty list is included as the last element of the list. As a more convenient notation, *list notation* can be used to represent lists. Elements are enclosed in square brackets and separated by commas.

> [X,Y,Z] .

Special notation to separate the head and tail in list notation is the vertical bar.

> [Head|Tail] .

A special use of list notation is the *string* where a series of characters is represented as a group by a list of the characters' ASCII codes.

PROGRAM COMPONENTS

A Prolog program is made up of *sentences*. A sentence has a *head* and *body* which are separated by colon/hyphen (:-) and ends with a period. Either the head or the body may be empty. The head contains at most one term and the body may contain more. A sentence may be viewed *declaratively* so that

> P :- Q,S.

means P is *true* if Q and S are true. A sentence may be viewed *procedurally* so that

> P :- Q,S.

means P is a *goal* which succeeds if the subgoals, Q and S succeed.

If the head of the sentence is not empty, the sentence is called a *clause*. If the body of a clause is empty it is called a *unit* clause and is written without the :-.

A sentence with an empty head is a *directive* specifically used for *questions* in which **?-** replaces **:-**.

There may be more than one clause with the same predicate for the head of the rule. Such multiple clauses allow alternatives for the rule. The group of one or more such clauses is called the *procedure* for that rule.

Prolog interpreters have some predicate definitions provided as part of the Prolog system. These definitions are known as *built-in predicates, built-in procedures* or *evaluable predicates*.

A significant number of the built-in predicates are *operators* used mainly for doing integer arithmetic in Prolog. Operators are assigned *precedence*, which is then used to determine which operation will be carried out first in the case of ambiguity.

PROLOG PROCESSING

In the *declarative semantics* of Prolog processing, the program attempts to prove the goal it has been given. The goal is or is not found *true*. A true *instance* of a goal is found by the success of the same goal in the head of a clause in the program. That clause's subgoals must succeed with any variables having been instantiated to the same constants as those in the goal.

Declaratively, Prolog processing *activates* the goal. Procedurally, Prolog processing *calls* the procedure or *executes* the goal.

The system starts at the top of the program and searches for a clause whose head *matches* or *unifies* with the goal so it can satisfy the goal. If a match is found, any goals in the body of the clause are executed in a manner like the first. Throughout the process, unification results in *instantiation* of variables. If some subgoal fails, *backtracking* is begun and variables are uninstantiated (in the reverse order), as necessary, so that attempts to resatisfy a goal or subgoal can be made.

FOUNDATION IN LOGIC

Prolog is based on a formal logic system called *predicate calculus*. The form of clauses in Prolog is that of *Horn clauses*, in that at most one atomic expression appears to the left of the :- sign. Prolog's processing uses *resolution* to carry out its tasks and follows a *depth-first* rather than *breadth-first* search strategy.

For further discussion of the formalisms and foundation of Prolog, see the articles and books listed in Appendix B, Further Reading.

Built-in Predicates
Typical of DECsystem-10/20 Prolog

Input and Output of Databases
consult(F)
Directs Prolog to augment the current database with facts and rules from the file named F. File names may have to be enclosed in single quote marks. If, during the reading of the database, an entry of the form

```
?- <predicate>
```

is read, it is immediately activated and succeeds or fails. In the database, entries are rearranged so that like predicates are grouped together but each appears in the group in the order it appeared. Shorthand notation for **consult**(file) is **[file]**. Several files may be consulted,

```
[file1,file2,file3].
```

reconsult(F)
Directs Prolog to read in the database as does consult, except that it replaces predicates in the database with new definitions for those predicates wherever the predicate name and number of arguments is the same. Shorthand form for reconsulting a file is **[-file]**.

asserta(C)
The clause, C, which may be a rule or fact, is added to the database at the top of the group of like predicates. Rules should be enclosed in an extra set of parentheses.

assertz(C)
Like asserta except the new predicate is added to the bottom of its group.

retract(C)
The first fact or predicate in the database that matches the clause, C, is erased from the database. The match must include the predicate name and the arity.

abolish(C,A)
Erases all instances of the clauses with the predicate name, C, and the number of arguments, A (called arity).

listing
Writes a copy of all the clauses in the database to the current output stream.

listing(N)
Writes a copy of the clauses with the predicate name, N, as their head to the current output stream.

Input and Output of Questions and Answers
read(X)
The next term from the current input stream is read and unified with X. The item in the input stream must end with a period followed by a space or a return. If the read finds the marker for the end of the input file, X is unified with a special value, varying depending on the system in use. Further attempt to read cause an error. Read can be used to check for a match as well as for input.

get0(Ch)
The next character from the input stream is accessed and Ch gets the value of the character's ASCII code. Can be used to check as well as input.

get(Ch)
Like get0 except the next non-blank printing character is gotten.

skip(Ch)
Reads and skips over characters until a match for Ch is found. Next get will read the next character.

ttyget0(Ch)
ttyget(Ch)
ttyskip(N)
Like get0, get and skip except the character is from the terminal (user).

write(X)
The term, X, is written to the current output stream. For arithmetic expressions, notation can be modified.

nl
A new line is started in the current output file.

tab(N)
N spaces are written into the current output file.

put(N)
The character whose ASCII code is the integer, N, is written to the current output stream.

display(T)
The term, T is output to the terminal screen in standard, prefix notation.

ttyput(N)
ttynl
ttyflush
Do character-based output to the terminal screen.

see(F)
The file named F becomes the current input stream. Reading will begin at the beginning of the file.

seeing(F)
F is unified with the name of the current input stream.

seen
Closes the current input stream. Reverts to file, user, if no other input stream specified.

tell(F)
The file named F becomes the current output stream. If F already had content, it will be erased.

telling(F)
F is unified with the name of the current output stream.

told
Closes the current output stream. Reverts to file user unless another output stream is specified.

close(F)
Closes file F, which could be either current input or output stream.

rename(F,N)
If file F is open, it is closed and given the new name, N. If N is [ ], the file is deleted.

nofileerrors
A mechanism that allows for graceful shut-down in case of file errors.

Processing Control
P,Q
The comma represents conjunction of the goals P and Q. It can be read as "and." Both P and Q must be true for P,Q to be true.

P;Q
The semicolon represents the disjunction of the goals P and Q. It can be read as "or." Either P or Q must be true for P;Q to be true. In Prolog, semicolons in the body of rules can be eliminated by using a multiple rule definition.

not(P) or **\+(P)**
If the goal, P, succeeds in the database then the goal not(P) fails. If the goal, P, fails, then not(P) succeeds.

true
Always succeeds.

fail
Always fails.

abort
Stop the current activity and exit to the command level of Prolog.

!
The cut symbol. Freezes all choices made since the activation of the parent goal of the clause with the cut in it. If backtracking reaches the cut, fail the parent goal.

repeat
Generates an infinite series of backtracking choices. Backtracking to a repeat gives processing a "new start" so goals following resatisfaction of a repeat are being satisfied, not re-satisfied.

Arithmetic Manipulations

X + Y
Integer addition where X and Y are integer expressions.

X − Y
Integer subtraction, X and Y are integer expressions.

X * Y
Integer multiplication, X and Y are integer expressions.

X / Y
Integer division, X and Y are integer expressions.

X mod Y
X modulo Y, the remainder from integer division.

[X]
Evaluates to the integer value if X is an integer. Since strings of characters, such as "Hi" are represented as a list of integer values (their ASCII codes) a single character can be used in arithmetic expressions as an integer constant.

A is X
The integer expression X is evaluated and the result is unified with A.

X =:= Y
The values of X and Y, evaluated, are equal.

X =\= Y
The values of X and Y, evaluated, are not equal.

X < Y
The value of X is less than the value of Y (X and Y evaluated).

X > Y
The value of X is greater than the value of Y (X and Y evaluated).

X =< Y
The value of X is less than or equal to the value of Y (X and Y evaluated).

X >= Y
The value of X is greater than or equal to the value of Y (X and Y evaluated)

Observing and Debugging Processing
log
Turns on the recording of all the user interaction at the terminal.

nolog
Turns off the logging of user interaction. Default is usually on.

ancestors(L)
The list, L, contains the ancestor goals for the current goal. They are listed oldest to most recent.

subgoal_of(G)
Behaves as though the list, L, from ancestors were searched for the specific goal given as G. Succeeds if the current goal is a subgoal of G.

debug
Turns on the gathering and recording of data so that the programmer can follow the processing and instantiation procedures for all or part of a Prolog program. Debugging facilities vary greatly from system to system.

Within debug, there are a number of control options One of the easiest for a novice to use is trace, which can be called directly.

trace
Displays to the user information on each activated goal during Prolog processing. The predicate, its constants and variables or instantiations are shown. See Chapter 10 for an example of a trace.

Manipulating Terms and Variables
This set of predicates looks at Prolog from one layer above. Here the components of a Prolog program are the objects that will be manipulated or examined.

var(X)
Tests whether X is currently an uninstantiated variable.

nonvar(X)
Tests whether X is currently an instantiated variable.

atom(X)
Tests whether X is currently instantiated to an atom (a constant of arity 0, not an integer).

integer(X)
Tests whether X is currently instantiated to an integer.

atomic(X)
Tests whether X is currently instantiated to either an atom or an integer. That is atomic(X) succeeds if either atom(X) or integer(X) succeeds.

functor(T,P,A)
Tests or provides a form for constructing a structure for predicates. T represents the structure with functor (predicate name) P and arity (number of arguments) A.

arg(N,S,A)
Used to access the Nth argument of structure S, with the argument returned in or checked against A.

X=..L
L is a list made up of the predicate name from X followed by the arguments in X. =. is pronounced univ.

X == Y
Checks whether the terms currently instantiated to X and Y are literally the same.

X \ = = Y
Checks whether the terms instantiated to X and Y are literally different.

call(X)
Activates X as a goal. Processing is carried out as if the goal itself had appeared where call(X) appeared.

X
Just the same as call(X), but not as communicative to a reader of the program.

name(X,L)
X is an atom or an integer, L is a list of ASCII codes for the characters in X. Thus L is a string representation of the atom or integer.

Manipulating Data Objects
X = Y
Prolog trys to match the terms X and Y, instantiating variables in them as necessary. If they can be matched the goal succeeds; otherwise it fails.

length(L,S)
If L is instantiated to a list of determinate length, S will be instantiated to its length.

sort(L1,L2)
The elements of the first list, L1, are sorted in order: numerical for integers; ASCII for atoms; oldest first for variables; arity and names for complex terms. Then any duplicate values are eliminated.

bagof(V,P,B)
This predicate gathers all the instances of the variable V that appear in goals, P, that are provable. It puts the instances into a list that is instantiated to the bag, B. If there are no instances, the goal fails.

setof(X,P,S)
This predicate works as though bagof had been followed by sort. That is, the elements in the list, S, are sorted and duplicates have been removed. Existential quantifiers can be used with **bagof** and **setof**. For example, bagof(X,A^B^C^one(A,B,C,X),B).

Answers to Exercises

Chapter 1

1.1.1   ate <food> <meal

1.1.2   ate <food> <meal> <day>

1.1.3   ate <food> <day> <meal>
ate <day> <food> <meal>
ate <day> <meal> <food>

1.1.4   july 1,2 school
july 3 rest
july 4 travel
july <weeks> <do>

1.2.1

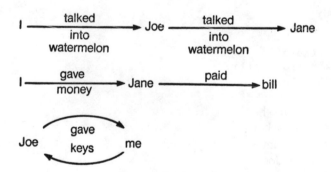

1.2.2   Note these are ambiguous. One might be "Joe gave the borrowed money to Sarah, who had owed some to Jane." "Joe borrowed money from Sarah; Jane had owed Sarah money too." My office is lighted by a window, cooled by an air conditioner and painted beige, which is a know of brown. In it I have a desk. I have the key that gives access to it.

1.3.1   Many choices <object> <does something>
<object> <is something>

1.3.2   Cool: sandals, shorts
Warm: sweaters, long sox
Nice gifts: flowers, sweaters

1.3.3   Not cool: sweaters, long sox, flowers
Not warm: sandals, shorts, flowers
Not nice gifts: sandals, shorts, long sox

1.4.1

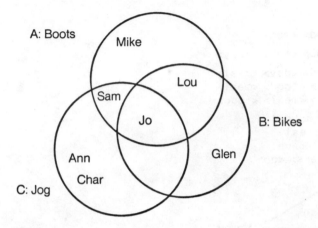

1.4.2   Jo, Lou

1.4.3   Jo

1.4.4   Mike, Sam, Jo, Lou, Glen

1.4.5   Everybody

Chapter 2

2.1.1   `on(book,table).`
`on(book,third_shelf).`
`owns(john,dog).`
`owns(jim,dog,black).`

2.1.2   Sarah is Jane's mother.
Sarah's mother is Jane.
Joe is father to Sam
Sam is father to Joe.

2.1.3   In this joke the word "nothing" means two different things in its two uses. Prolog would assume it means the same thing at all times.

2.2.1   (Facts as above)
`?- on(book,Where).`
`?- on(What,third_shelf).`
`?- owns(john,What).`
`?- owns(jim,dog,Color).`

2.2.2   `Thief = john`
`A = dog`
`Breed = jersey`

2.2.3   Breed is a meaningful name, which A is not. Thief is meaningful but may not convey the meaning intended.

2.3.1
```
What = call_agent;
What = write_home;
no
What = get_money;
What = study;
no
When = thursday;
When = tuesday;
no
```

2.3.2   seven plus "no"

2.4.1
```
Day = friday   Task = get_tickets
```

2.4.2
```
?- do(__,study).
```

2.4.3
```
?- do(When,What),do(When,study).
```

Chapter 3

3.1.1
```
no
```

3.1.2
```
wear(shorts) :- high(seventies).
```

3.1.3
```
plan(picnic) :- rain(none).
```

3.2.1
```
Day = sunday;
Day = tuesday;
Day = wednesday;
no
```

3.2.2
```
take(umbrella,Day) :- weather(Day,rainy).
```

3.2.3
```
take(umbrella,Day) :- weather(Day,overcast).
```

3.3.1
```
mixed_feelings(birders,Day) :- weather(Day,rainy),
              active(birds,Day).
```

3.3.2   it won't

3.4.1
```
Whom = bet;
Whom = cat;
no
Whom = bet;
Whom = cat;
no
Who = ann;
Who = abe;
no
```

3.4.2
```
?- married(Her,Him).
?- mother(__,Person),father(__,Person).
```

3.5.1   same responses as above plus
```
Younger = bet   Older = abe;
Younger = cat   Older = abe;
Younger = may   Older = abe;
Younger = nan   Older = abe;
no
```

3.5.2
```
glump(joe,sally).
glump(sam,joe).
glump(may,joe).
glump(leo,may).
glump(sister,leo).
knows(sally).
knows(Person) :- glump(Teach,Person), knows(Teacher).
```

3.6.1 Some answers will be reported, then Prolog will run out of internal space.

3.6.2 An oscillating recursion is set up with mother and father.
One or the other of these rules should not be included.

Chapter 4

4.1.1 Seven

4.1.2 Prolog will not be aware of any problem or contradiction.

4.2.1 Four values as we still have the duplicate for friday.

4.2.2
```
Outlook = rainy;
Outlook = fair;
no
```

4.3.1
```
Footgear = shoes   Hue = black;
Footgear = shoes   Hue = white;
Footgear = sneakers   Hue = red;
Footgear = skates   Hue = white;
Footgear = running_shoes   Hue = black:
no
```

4.3.2 All the earlier responses would be given, plus a set that report Footgear = sox for each color of sox, too. Because Prolog is simply matching on the pattern, sox are the same as footgear in the same predicate and a duplicated match can be found by searching for the same predicate twice.

4.4.1
```
happy(birders,When) ?
weather(When,fair) ?
active(birds,sunday) ?
happy(birders,sunday)
When = sunday ;
happy(birders,sunday) ?
active(birds,sunday) ?
weather(sunday,fair) ?
active(birds,tuesday) ?
When = tuesday ;
happy(birders,tuesday) ?
active(birds,tuesday) ?
weather(tuesday,fair) ?
active(birds,wednesday) ?
active(birds,wednesday)
happy(birders,wednesday)
```

```
        When = wednesday ;
         happy(birders,wednesday) ?
         active(birds,wednesday) ?
         weather(wednesday,fair) ?
         weather(When,fair)
         happy(birders,When)
        no
```

4.4.2   The first match attempted would be to color(eyes,Hue,Person) which
        would instantiate Sue, then sky color would be sought for the next
        match. After all these, other matches for the first part would be sought
        (there are none).

4.5.1
```
        ancestor(Older,Younger).
        parent(Older,Younger).
        mother(Older,Younger).
        mother(ann,Younger).
        mother(ann,bet).
        Older = ann   Younger = bet
```

4.5.2
```
        Younger = bet,   Older = ann ;
        Younger = may,   Older = bet ;
        Younger = cat,   Older = ann ;
        Younger = nan,   Older = may ;
        Younger = bet,   Older = abe ;
        Younger = cat,   Older = abe ;
        Younger = may,   Older = ann ;
        Younger = nan,   Older = ann ;
        Younger = nan,   Older = bet ;
        Younger = may,   Older = abe ;
        Younger = nan,   Older = abe ;
        no
```

Chapter 5

5.1.1   [red,orange,yellow,green,blue,indigo,violet]

5.1.2   rainbow([red,orange,yellow,green,blue,indigo,violet]).

5.1.3
```
        ?-rainbow(__,__,__,__,__,__,violet]).
        ?-rainbow(__,__,__,__,__,__,purple]).
```

5.2.1
```
        Head = red   Tail = [orange,yellow]
        Head = red   Tail = [orange]
        Head = red   Tail = [ ]
        none; the empty list has no head nor tail
```

5.2.2
```
        Head = k_wilhelm   Tail = [juniper_time,fault_lines];
        Head = u_leguin    Tail = [left_hand_of_darkness];
        no
```

5.2.3   ?- author([Name|__]).

5.3.1
```
        Element = k_wilhelm
        List = [k_wilhelm,juniper_time,fault_lines];
        Element = juniper_time
        List = [k_wilhelm,juniper_time,fault_lines];
        Element = fault_lines
        List = [k_wilhelm,juniper_time,fault_lines];
        Element = u_leguin
        List = [u_leguin,left_hand_of_darkness];
```

```
                Element = left_hand_of_darkness
                List = [u_leguin,left_hand_of_darkness];
                Element = l_m_alcott
                List = [l_m_alcott,little_women];
                Element = little_women
                List = [l_m_alcott,little_women];
                no
```

5.3.2   `?- author(What).`

5.4.1   `List = [k_wilhelm,juniper_time,fault_lines]`
        `List = [u_leguin,left_hand_of_darkness]`
        `List = [l_m_alcott,little_women]`

5.4.2   `clean_cut(Dwarf) :- dwarves(List1), no_beard(List2),`
        `                member(Dwarf,List1), member(Dwarf,List2).`

5.4.3   `What = condor;`
        `What = cardinal;`
        `What = crane;`
        `What = bluebird;`
        `What = sparrow;`
        `(user interrupt)`

5.5.1   Use third_place, as it implies at least two books.

5.5.2   `author_names(Which) :- author(List), front(Which,List).`

5.5.3   `?- rainbow(List),last(violet,List).`
        `?- rainbow(List),last(purple,List).`

5.6.1   `List = [condor,crane,sparrow]`
        `Result = [frigate_bird,condor,crane,sparrow];`
        `List = [bluebird,cardinal]`
        `Result = [frigate_bird,bluebird,cardinal];`
        `no`
        `List = [bluebird,cardinal]   What = [bluebird];`
        `no`
        `List = [condor,crane,sparrow]`
        `Result = [condor,crane,sparrow,condor,crane,sparrow];`
        `List = [bluebird,cardinal]`
        `Result = [bluebird,cardinal,bluebird,cardinal];`
        `no`
        `L1 = [condor,crane,sparrow]`
        `L2 = [bluebird,cardinal]`
        `Result = [condor,crane,sparrow,bluebird,cardinal];`
        `no`

5.6.2   `List = [condor,crane,sparrow]`
        `Result = [sparrow,crane,condor];`
        `List = [bluebird,cardinal]`
        `Result = [cardinal,bluebird];`
        `no`
        `List = [condor,crane,sparrow]`
        `Result = [condor,crane,sparrow,sparrow,crane,condor];`
        `List = [bluebird,cardinal]`
        `Result = [bluebird,cardinal,cardinal,bluebird];`
        `no`
        `no (none of the rarebird lists is a palindrome)`

5.6.3   `odd_pal(Half,Result) :- append(Half,Tail,Result),`
        `                reverse(Half,[H|Tail]).`

5.7.1
```
H = one      T = [[two]]
H = [one]    T = [[two]]
H = [one]    T = [two]
H = one      T = [[two,three]]
H = one      T = [two,[three]]
H = one      T = [two,three]
```

5.7.2
```
H = two      T = [one]
H = [two]    T = [[one]]
```

Chapter 6

6.1.1   Descriptively: your paragraph should use the terms "defined" and "is related to" or such expressions that concern the meaning of the rules. Prescriptively: your paragraph should use terms like "process", talk about the order things happen, or express the idea of change over time.

6.1.2

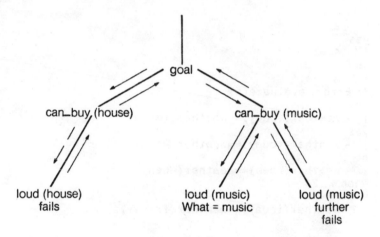

6.2.1
```
ancestor(Old,Young) :- parent(Old,Young)
ancestor(Old,Young) :-
     ancestor(Old,Mid),parent(Mid,Young)
ancestor(Old,Young) :- parent(Old,Young).
ancestor(Old,Young) :-
     parent(Mid,Young),ancestor(Old,Mid).
```
The second is preferable because it controls the recursion.

6.2.2
```
parent(joe,sam).
parent(sam,jay).
parent(jay,rod).
parent(rod,lou).
ancestor(Old,Young) :- parent(Old,Young).
ancestor(Old,Young) :-
     parent(Mid,Young),ancestor(Old,Mid).
descendant(Y,O) :- parent(O,Y).
descendant(Y,O) :- descendant(Y,M),parent(O,M).
(or descendant(Y,O) :- ancestor(O,Y).)
```

6.3.1 `When = tuesday;`
`no`

6.3.2 `When = tuesday;`
`no`

6.3.3 `holiday(friday,july_4).`

6.4.1 `order(Vegetable) :- green(Vegetable),!,fail.`
`order(Vegetable).`

6.4.2 `isnt(some_goal) :- call(some_goal),!,fail.`
`isnt(some_goal).`

Chapter 7

7.1.1 Input and output streams are a series of sequential characters. Since sequence is critical, so is time, and work over time is more of a procedural concept than a definitional concept.

7.1.2
```
| ?- A==A.
A = _22
yes
| ?- A==a.
no
| ?- A=:=a.
** Error: evaluate(a)
no
| ?- weather(today)==weather(today).
yes
| ?- weather(today)==weather(When).
no
| ?- weather(When)==weather(When).
When = _24
yes
| ?- weather(today)==weather(friday).
no
```

7.2.1 `similar(Days) :- bagof(D,weather(D,Outlook),Days).`

7.2.2 `forcast(Plan) :- bagof(D,Outlook^`
`(weather(D,Outlook)),Plan).`

7.2.3 `summary(Plan) :- setof(D,Outlook^`
`(weather(D,Outlook)),Plan).`

7.2.4 `kinds(Number) :- summary(Plan), length(Plan,Number).`

Chapter 8

8.1.1 `rulea :- reconsult(rulefile).`
rulefile contains a new rulea (also with no argments).

8.1.2 `rule1 :- abolish(rule1,0).`
`rule2(X) :- abolish(rule2,1).`
`rule3 :- retract(rule3).`

8.1.3 `same(up,down) :- abolish(same,2).`

8.2.1 `consult(rulefile).`
rulefile contains the question including the ?- in front of it so it acts as
ən immediate directive

8.2.2   `do :- see(file3),read(Item),seen,consult(Item).`
        `?- do.`

8.3.1   add to the rules in the text:
        `birthday:- show(['What',month,is,your,'birthday?']),`
        `read(Month),`
        `respond(Month).`
        `respond(november) :- show(['That"s', this,month]).`
        `respond(M) :- show(['That"s,a,while,yet]).`

8.3.2   `show([ ]).`
        `go :- process(Outlook),show(['Outlook:']),`
           `write(Outlook),nl.`

8.4.1   `do :- see(file1), tell(file2),`
           `repeat,get(Ch),process(Ch),seen,told.`
        `process(Ch) :- end_of_file(Ch).`
        `process(Ch) :- put(Ch), fail.`

8.4.2   `do :- see(file1),get(C1),get(C2),get(C3),seen,`
        `+\([C1,C2,C3] = "HAL"), abort.`

Chapter 9

9.1.1   20
        26
        14

9.1.2   `do(X,Y,Z) :-`
                  `X is (2) + (3 * 4 + 6),`
                  `Y is (2 + 3) * 4 + 6,`
                  `Z is (2 + 3 * 4) + 6 mod 2.`

9.2.1   `facts of the form temp(high,<value>).`
        `ave_high(Val) :- bagof(Each,temp(high,Each),Bg),`
                  `length(Bg,Num), sum(Bg,Sm),`
                  `Val = Sm / Num.`

9.2.2   `double(Old,Young) :- person(Old,O_age),person(Young,Y_age),`
                  `O_age =:= (Y_age * 2).`

9.2.3   `age_plus_ten(Subject) :- person(Subject,Age),!,`
                  `person(Other,Other_age),`
                  `Other_age > Age+10,`
                  `write(Other), fail.`

9.3.1   Switch the $>=$ sign for $=<$

9.3.2   Duplicate values would be placed before the existing value instead of after it. The result would be the same.

9.3.3   It will work on characters in strings as numbers.

9.3.4   It will work on constant names, sorting them alphabetically.

Chapter 10

10.1.1

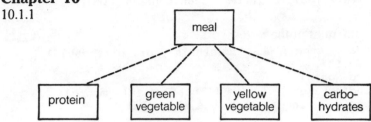

10.1.2

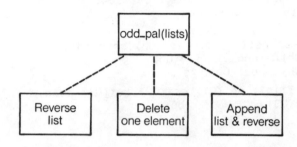

10.1.3   ```val id_paln(L) :- palindrome(Half,L)
val id_paln(L) :- odd_pal(Part,L).```

10.2.1   Machine trace of this program is shown in Experimenting with Chapter 5.

10.2.2   ```?- reverse([a,b],R).
?- append([a,b],[x,y],R]).
?-palindrome([ ],R).```

10.3.1   These are the previous rules for reverse,append and palindrome. The components of the mutiple rules should be grouped together. Names that are more communicative should be used.

10.3.2   ```have_groceries :- stock(starch),
        stock(protein),stock(sweets).
stock(starch) :- cereal(Brand),supper_dish(Pasta).
stock(protein) :- sandwich(Filling),milk(white).
stock(sweets) :- juice(Fruit),pie(Type).```

10.3.3   ```stock(sweets) :- juice(Fruit),pie(Type),+\(Fruit = Type).```

INDEXES

General Index

Throughout the General Index, bold face indicates built-in predicates. The Index to Built-in Predicates follows (see page 221). The Index to Examples appears separately on page 223.

Index to Built-in Predicates

Index to Examples